Embodying
God

EMBODYING GOD

IN COLONIES OF
HEAVEN ON EARTH

BOYD W. MORRIS

BASILEIA
PUBLISHING

Basileia Publishing
P.O. Box 60695
Colorado Springs, CO 80960

© 2015 Boyd W. Morris

All rights reserved. No part of this book may be reproduced in any form without written permission from Basileia Publishing.

Basileia Publishing is the publishing arm of Basileia, a global expression of the Church in ecclesiastical fellowship with *Communio Christiana*. Basileia (which means "kingdom") imagines, cultivates and launches kingdomcultural communities and initiatives, embodying God in colonies of heaven on earth. For more information, write Basileia, P.O. Box 60695, Colorado Springs, CO 80960, or visit www.basileians.com.

All Scripture citations are from the English Standard Version, unless noted otherwise.

ISBN-10: 1519604874
ISBN-13: 978-1519604873

To all who dare to form communities
where people belong to believe.

We are a colony of heaven.

Philippians 3:20
(Moffat Translation)

Contents

Foreword 9
Preface 13
Acknowledgments 25
Introduction 27
   1 Embodying God 34
   2 The Empire of God 46
   3 The Politics of Worship 53
   4 The Physics of Spirituality 60
   5 Game On! 65
   6 The Drug of Immortality 71
   7 Project Elrond 76
   8 A Great Music 84
   9 Change Your World 90
  10 Waybread of Elves 94
  11 Circle Me, Lord 103
  12 Jane Austen Rules! 108
  13 Colony of Heaven 113

14	What's Your Value?	117
15	Something Big's Happening	122
16	Dangerous Paths Taken	128
17	Faith in Humanity	132

Afterword 138
About the Author 142

Foreword

SO LET ME ASK YOU a couple of questions.

Is the Church a religious club or a colony of heaven on earth? Is it a Sunday-focused religious society or a living, breathing colony that lives a full-orbed and multifaceted life seven days a week?

In *Embodying God*, Boyd Morris calls us to embrace the Church at its fundamental local level as a *colony*.

On a grander scale, he calls us to embrace the Church universal both as a kingdom and as the City of God.

On a personal level, he challenges each of us to be what God has made us to be with grace, gusto, and courage.

The colony Boyd has in mind is one graced by the bracing air of heaven's low hanging clouds. Jesus is in those clouds, you see, and colonists have their heads in them. They also have their feet planted firmly on the earth, which is in keeping with the heaven-to-earth trajectory of the kingdom petition in the Lord's Prayer.

Embodying God

A Christian colony's foundation is that of Christ and the apostles. Its light is the Lamb. Its people are the blood-bought people of the Lamb. Its families are its basic unit. Its call is to worship and work and do God's will on earth.

I was raised in a Christian colony. Its name, translated from the language of its European founders, means "glory." I was raised in "Glory." It was a micro-civilization that modeled the macro-civilization the Church is called to be. We worshiped and worked in "Glory," and we took on the world. I could tell you stories.

Do you want to change the shape of a country or continent for the better? Start with a colony. I offer as evidence the Pilgrims who landed at Plymouth Rock in 1620. A nation arose from that colony.

Colonization isn't a new idea.

Adam and Eve's original call was to colonize the earth. The Great Commission aims at the Christian re-colonization of the planet. The father of Western Civilization was a colonizing monk named Benedict (480-543). Between AD 400 and AD 800, Celtic monks built one thousand communities in Ireland and the British Isles. As one author put it, those colonies saved civilization.

To become what it should be, today's world needs Christian colonies. That's why I think *Embodying God* is so important. Its narrative blueprint points the way forward.

Foreword

Enjoy. But be warned. It might ruin you for Sunday-only religion.

William Paul Mikler
Archbishop, *Communio Christiana*

Preface

When it comes to embodying God, believing is seeing, and we must belong to believe.

Over this last year, I've been on a peculiar, dangerous, and wonderful journey of exploring a way of belonging to believe that embodies God. Each chapter of this book revolves around questions I've been asking about the who, what, when, where, how, and why of embodying God.

Another word for "journey" is "quest," which is the root of the word *question*. While it's true that questions call us to search and research for answers, putting it this way takes all the fun out of it. So let's turn it around by recognizing that what we love more than anything is the search itself, the journey, the adventure, the adrenaline rush of discovering what's over the next hill. We start asking really good questions only *after* our feet set out the door.

The truth is, answers bore me. So do questions asked out of a mortal, scribal mentality that sits comfortably at home theorizing about this and that even while politely keeping open the possibility of going on an actual adventure someday.

Embodying God

But high-spirited adventurers who've already left the comfort of the couch ask outrageous questions—peculiar questions, dangerous questions, wonderful questions. Questions don't birth quests. Quests birth great questions, the kind worth bantering back and forth together on the road and in the quiet places we find to rest along the way.

It's like what Bilbo says to Gandalf in *The Fellowship of the Ring* (2001 movie): "I want to see mountains again, *mountains*, Gandalf. And then find somewhere quiet where I can finish my book." Amen, Bilbo.

I'm on a quest to form colonies of heaven that embody God on earth. What a mountain! What a glorious quest! As a result, the questions I hear coming out of my mouth make me laugh out loud at times because they're so outrageous. Polite society is embarrassed by such behavior, but then I've never had much love for polite society. I'd rather eat rations on the way to New Jerusalem than feast in Babylon.

BELIEVING IS SEEING

The adage, "seeing is believing" is thoroughly mistaken. It's exactly backward.

Did you know that our eyes supply only about 15% of what we think we see? Our brains supply the rest from a vast database of imagery stored therein. The peculiar truth is that we see what we *believe* should be there, not necessarily what *is* there. For example, go to YouTube and watch, "The Rotating Mask Illusion." Watch as the bulging (convex) face on the mask turns until you now see the other (concave) side of the mask. Your mind's eye overrides your physical eyes and

Preface

reconstructs the concave image to look like a normal (convex) face. Believing is seeing.

We carry around inside us an immense storehouse of beliefs that comprise our *feel* for the world. We start forming this feel as babies, crawling around on the floor *feeling* and touching everything in reach. Feeling and touching things creates a concrete picture of the world that gets stored up inside us. Then, throughout our life, our brains draw upon this storehouse—this feel for the world—to form the images in our mind's eye that we call *seeing*.

When the disciples saw the resurrected Jesus with their physical eyes, they couldn't believe it. So Jesus said to them, "Touch me, and see" (Lk. 24:39).

Jesus didn't lecture His disciples to believe. No amount of *information* would ever open their eyes. The disciples didn't need information; they needed *formation*. They needed to *touch* Jesus' body and *reform* their internal database to comport with the new reality of things transformed by the accomplished fact of the resurrection. To see the new world of the Kingdom of God they *first* needed to touch the form of a resurrected human body embodying God.

So how do *we* do it?

How do we *touch* Christ, who in the Incarnation became humanity clothed in divinity so that we might embody God in our humanity? Exactly, how does *that* work?

We must belong.

Embodying God

BELONG TO BELIEVE

We touch, feel and belong, pretty much in that order, and only then do we believe.

It's vain to require people to believe to belong. This flawed approach doesn't work because it just doesn't feel right. Belief that feels right comes when we exercise not only our physical sense of touch but also by touching realities embodied in *story*.

We're made with a divine capacity to go beyond being mere scribal observers of great epic stories. We each have a unique God-given ability to become actors and participants in the stories themselves, enabling us both to be touched by and to put our touch on stories.

To touch and to be touched are things *done*, not just things thought or said. I watched *Batman Begins* (again) last night. In Bruce Wayne's journey to becoming Batman, he comes to the realization, "It's not who I am underneath, but what I *do* that defines me." Underneath, we're all created in God's image and likeness. That's our nature. Okay. Now, let's set that awesome potential free by acts of total baptismal emersion into story-formed worlds.

For example, I *feel* like I *belong* on the Starship Enterprise and Sheila feels like she belongs in Jane Austen's world. I'm also quite at home in Tolkien's Middle-earth. Sheila and I are baptized into these worlds and belong to them. Requiring belief before baptism is backward, producing "converts," not disciples. Baptism rightly practiced is a rite of passage by which we belong to believe.

Preface

Sheila and I, each in our unique way, having been baptized into the story-formed worlds of Star Trek, Jane Austen, and Middle-earth, feel *touched* by the people, places and events of these worlds. But even more, as we get lost in these stories we *put our touch on them*, adorning each with imagery, sounds, smells, and a feel of things of our individual making. We become actors in and co-creators of the stories themselves.

Good actors don't just *imitate* the characters they portray; they *embody* them. The word "character" is related to the word "charism." A charism is a divine gift, a God-given capacity, a way of embodying God. Jesus said something peculiar about John the Baptist. "If you are willing to accept it," Jesus said, John the Baptist "is Elijah" (Matt. 11:14). Of course, John and Elijah were two distinct people who lived in two distinct times and places. However, Jesus wasn't emphasizing what distinguished them, but rather what they had in *common*. They mystically shared the same divine charism, the same power of *action* whose source is in God. John the Baptist and Elijah *belonged* to each other as spiritual brothers who both embodied God in a similar way.

Colonies of heaven on earth contain spiritual brothers and sisters who belong to each other and embody God in a common way because they all mystically share a *common* charism. They're all char-actors in the same play. Likewise, musicians, each with their distinct charisms, shine most brightly when their individual instruments combine into a Great Music, creating a symphonic story greater than the sum of its parts. God embodies Himself in such stories.

To *act in concert* as high-spirited human creators in the likeness of the Creator God in whose image we are is not just an outward, superficial imitation of God, but the *act* of embodying God.

Embodying God is basic to all that it means to be human. God ordained it this way when He made us in His image and likeness. Because God alone is the source of all high-spirited human creativity, embodying God is not something that we must work for, but the starting point that we work from. Now, the only question is whether we're going to embody God in colonies of heaven on earth or remain advocates of or captives in colonies of hell on earth.

The so-called "real" world is the twisted creation of *unsanctified* high-spirited human creativity misdirected to nefarious ends. In contrast, the Kingdom of God, the alternative to the so-called "real" world, invites its citizens and guests to belong and embody God in colonies of *sanctified* high-spirited human creativity. Individuals here are free to play their respective parts in accord with the community's overall shared charism and thereby create worlds of wonder.

Creating Worlds of Wonder

Over this past year I've done something that some might consider a bit misguided, if not outright dangerous—I've immersed myself in *mythology*, not so much by studying it, but by *experiencing* it. I've been running an experiment of sorts, curious how my feel for the "real" world might change if I totally and thoroughly immersed myself by baptism into secondary, imaginative worlds.

What I've discovered is wonderfully alarming. As I touch and feel the touch of the characters, places, and epic events of the

Preface

secondary worlds of great stories, these worlds take on a more real sense to me than what polite society (remember those people?) call the "real" world.

The divinely granted human ability to create and then immerse ourselves in secondary or alternative worlds is the essential skill we must cultivate in our quest to dismantle the insanity of the "real" world and restore all things.

A sanctified capacity to imagine and *belong* to secondary worlds is vital to advancing the Kingdom of God on earth. Thus, it's problematic calling secondary worlds "mythological" because to those with *sanctified* imaginations such worlds are real—more real than the Fallen World System, which is a world passing away like a wisp of fog at sunrise.

What mortals in the "real" world denounce as "mythology" is, in fact, the God-given raw material that sanctified immortals use in making all things new.

What is the *true* real world anyhow? Jesus says there are those who "see" with their eyes but who do "not perceive" the true reality of things (Mk. 4:12). He also speaks of others to whom the mystery (i.e., the secret counsel) of the Kingdom of God is given (Mk 4:11). Of these Jesus says, "blessed are your eyes, for they see" (Matt. 13:16).

The mystery or secret counsel of which Jesus speaks is not a concept but a *community* to which we're all destined to belong. Populating this community are angels and archangels and the spirits of just men made perfect, a pantheon of beings (i.e., of gods) who share a common, divinely inspired, story-formed mythological consciousness flowing with the power of sanctified imagination able to create the secondary, imaginative worlds of which they dream. The members of this community share a common mystical connection with each other via the energies of God—dimensions of God's charism, which He in turn shares with humanity—energies able to unite us as a *collective* body who then embody God in and across the expanses of space and time.

IT'S JUST COMMON SENSE

Every individual has his or her *individual* sense of things. But only a body of people who share a common mystical connection with each other can exercise *common* sense.

Common sense emerges when individuals unite in using their senses in a common way, beginning with the sense of touch. By touching the same realities with our *collective* imagination, that is, by becoming actors in the same story, we begin to share a common charism, which *forms* us into a body.

Evangelistic, pastoral, and teaching meetings that equip and *inform* individuals are good as far as they go, but they don't go far enough. Forming individuals into a body requires baptismal immersion into a *shared* mythology that unites us in a common vision and experience of the mystical connections between all things in Christ.

For example, there is a mystical connection between the *physical* body of Christ, the *Church* as the Body of Christ, and the *bread* of the Eucharistic worship of the Church as the body of Christ. All three are the body of Christ, each more the same than different. It's just common sense.

Preface

"Touch me, and see," Jesus says. How? Common sense tells us there are three ways to touch Jesus and see. We can touch Jesus' physical body, or the Church, or the bread in communion since all three are the body of Christ. Getting comfortable with common sense equivalencies like this is the key to embodying God in colonies of heaven on earth.

I trust you'll find plenty of common sense in this book.

THE KINGDOMCULTURAL ALTERNATIVE

Speaking of common sense, Tolkien and Lewis were modern masters.

Tolkien was a devout Catholic whose good friend, C.S. Lewis, was a devout Anglican. Both men were on a mission to open the eyes, not just of individuals, but of their *people*—the English—to the true real world. When the Church as a body loses her collective imagination, then the forms, rituals, ceremonies, and structures of the Church become an empty shell. We lose the story's meaning. The common charism that mystically unites us remains unseen. We have eyes but do not see. People then leave the Church to find a community (a body) of heroes who yet dare to imagine new worlds. Then the nations that such expressions of the Church seek to disciple also start to lose steam, resulting in civilization-wide collapse. But Tolkien and Lewis didn't just stand by and watch their people and culture collapse; they had a *feel* of something at the core of the Christian faith that could be revived—the art form of a people *collectively touching God embodied in a mystical communion of heroes of myth and legend.*

Embodying God

Let's become as babies touching the world as for the first time and rediscover the universal language of myth and legend. The language of myth and legend is like the nerve impulses of a body that enable the body's members to speak to one another and function as one. Myth and legend happen when a symphony's individual musicians synchronize their respective parts according to a common score. The language of myth and legend is the language of actors in the drama of making all things new.

Civilizations collapse. Even collective bodies as great as Egypt and Rome die. But death is not the end. In times when civilizations collapse, it is then that old things, which turn out not to be old, but *universal*, get rediscovered afresh. We live in exciting times.

This book emerged out of my quest to touch secondary, imaginative worlds. I seek to kindle my passion and ability, and that of my people, the Church, to dare and re-imagine all over again how we as the Church are on the greatest of quests—the quest of embodying God in colonies of heaven on earth.

Ironically, I've come to see how we are often more awake to the possibilities of embodying God when we sleep and dream than when we're awake. Thus, we must create bridges between the substance of our dreams and our waking state. I offer the chapters of this book as a few of the stones for building such a bridge.

The creation of secondary, imaginative worlds is vital to learning how to use the resurrection tools Christ has already given His Church (such as the Liturgy) to create the

Preface

alternative world of kingdomculture. Kingdomculture is resurrection culture, the genuine alternative to the "real" world.

I consider my experimental immersion into mythology this past year as something akin to an athlete training for the Olympics. As Tolkien said in a letter to Milton Waldman in 1951,

> I believe that legends and myths are largely made of 'truth', and indeed present aspects of it that can only be received in this mode; and long ago certain truths and modes of this kind were discovered and must always reappear.

"Touch me, and see," says Jesus. Ready to indulge is some sanctified imagination? Ready to touch and experience something peculiar, dangerous, and wonderful?

Boyd W. Morris
Colorado Springs, Colorado
Feast of Christ the King, 2015

Acknowledgments

THIS BOOK IS THE FRUIT of many conversations with a host of people in a diversity of settings.

I've conversed with Sheila about the inklings in this book more than with anyone else—over dinner, on the way to the airport, first thing in the morning (but not before she's had coffee), and on the back deck when the weather's nice. The rough edges remaining in these meditations exist, not because she didn't try to smooth them out, but because I'm still learning how to listen.

My friend and fellow-Presbyter, John Hunt and I have a wonderful weekly habit of getting together to test out the things we're writing on each other before daring to print them. Sharpened and inspired by John's feedback, I completed most of these meditations within twenty-four hours of our weekly summits.

Bishop William Mikler, who graciously agreed to write the Foreword, encouraged me to compile these meditations and get them published. Additionally, several months ago, in the middle of one of our regular video chats, something electric happened as we started pondering the metaphor of the

Embodying God

Church as a colony of heaven. Within a few days I wrote the lead piece that is now Chapter 1 of this book, "Embodying God," a pithy phrase that also serves as this book's title. This book in general and Chapter 1 in particular are a kind of roadmap that Bishop Mikler, my fellow Basileians, and I are using in our efforts to embody God in colonies of heaven on earth.

Finally, I've received so much affirmation and great feedback from readers of my *Secret Counsel* blog series where these meditations first appeared. Thank you for engaging with me on the journey and thereby elevating these meditations into an ongoing conversation into which we can now include an even wider circle of fellow pilgrims.

> *I was glad when they said to me,*
> *"Let us go to the house of the Lord!"*
>
> (Psalm 122:1a)

Introduction

Embodying God in colonies of heaven on earth is divinely human.

Each chapter of this book explores what happens when humanity and divinity intersect in

- Community life (Chapter 1)
- Eucharistic worship (Chapter 2)
- Politics (Chapter 3)
- Science (Chapter 4)
- Sports (Chapter 5)
- Communion bread (Chapter 6)
- Space exploration (Chapter 7)
- Mythology (Chapter 8)
- Singing (Chapter 9)
- Sacraments (Chapter 10)
- Celtic prayer (Chapter 11)
- Romantic fiction (Chapter 12)
- Immigrant populations (Chapter 13)
- Life coaching (Chapter 14)
- Honest questions (Chapter 15)
- Hollywood movies (Chapter 16)
- Healing of our past (Chapter 17)

Embodying God

In these intersections of humanity and divinity the future becomes present, the Church prevails while the gates of Hades do not, the Kingdom of God replaces the Fallen World System, the dead are raised, the lion lays down with the lamb, evil is exhausted, and the creation no longer groans in bondage to decay.

Such vast cosmic phenomena don't just happen to other people in far away times and places; they happen to you and to me each day. I promise you. All that's required to see such happenings is a little imagination. These human-divine intersections are surprisingly near at hand and pervasive.

And so, over this last year I exercised a little imagination of my own in writing the chapters of this book, which began as meditations on the Scripture during our Abbey of St. John worship services. I then further developed each meditation in the *Secret Counsel* blog series I write. Thus, under each chapter title, I've noted the point in the Church Year when these imaginative intersections of the human and divine occurred. Dating the chapters this way elevates them somehow. Perhaps it's because it anchors them to the bedrock of the larger conversation of the Communion of Saints across the ages.

Each chapter in its unique way testifies to a glorious truth—the veil between heaven and earth is quite *thin*. Colonies of heaven on earth embody God in thin places where heaven and earth kiss and humanity and divinity intersect. So, it's only appropriate that in Chapter 1, "Embodying God," I describe a vision of a colony of heaven on earth that I'm presently building with my fellow Basileians.

Introduction

A colony of heaven on earth is a microcosm of the Kingdom of God, which I'm fond of also calling "The Empire of God," as I do in Chapter 2. Since the Kingdom of God is an empire and worshippers are at the heart of all empires, this chapter explores why the "Roman Empire didn't have a problem with Christian believers, but with Christian *worshipers*" (p. 46).

And just so we don't think that the head on collision between the Empire of God and the prodigal empires of the Fallen World System are a thing of the past, I wrote Chapter 3, "The Politics of Worship." Here, we pull back the curtain on what truly caused the fall of the former Soviet Union. Embodying God is as political as it gets.

Embodying God is also as mysterious as it gets because the spirituality of the Kingdom of God is a resurrected *embodied* spirituality. So in Chapter 4, "The Physics of Spirituality," we'll have a little fun pondering the intersection of Word made flesh in Jesus' physical body, the Church, and in the bread of the Eucharist.

Trophies in the form of a cup are common throughout the world of sports. But why a cup? In Chapter 5, "Game On!" we explore this question. "It doesn't matter if you're sailing a boat, smacking a tennis ball, kicking a football, climbing 8,000-meter peaks, playing chess, or drinking Christ's blood from a chalice served by a priest in the Eucharistic worship of the Church. We're all playing the same game for the same prize" (p. 69). The prize? Embodying God, of course.

After reading this book, you'll probably think that the only thing I do other than write is watch movies, which wouldn't be far from the truth. In Chapter 6, "The Drug of Immortality," I reference four movies, including *Lucy*, all themed around embodying godlike powers with the aid of drugs. But what's wild is that two days before watching *Lucy* I was shocked to read one of the ancient Church Fathers, a disciple of the Apostle John, talking about what he calls "the drug of immortality," which made watching *Lucy* all the more interesting.

Speaking of movies, have you seen *The Martian*? I've only seen it twice (so far). Chapter 7, "Project Elrond," takes its name from a secret counsel scene in *The Martian* that takes its cue from one of my favorite secret counsel scenes of all time in *The Fellowship of the Ring*—the Council of Elrond. The theme of secret counsel not only appears in this chapter but constantly pops up throughout this book because it's at the heart of how we go about embodying God in colonies of heaven on earth.

In addition to watching movies and writing, I still get around to reading now and then. I wrote Chapter 8, "A Great Music," in the midst of reading *The Silmarillion*, Tolkien's foundational myth and legend underneath the more widely known myth and legend of *The Hobbit* and *The Lord of the Rings*. Over the years, I've struggled to give expression to the vital role of secret counsel in the mystery and miracle of embodying God. "But I'm now discovering in myth and legend a power of language, thought, and perception that liberates the wonder of *secret counsel*, the *mystery* of the kingdom, and the *sacraments* of the Church to operate as portals of transfiguration" (p. 85).

Introduction

Embodying God is a quest we pursue in a war zone. "Both the Kingdom of God and the Kingdom of Satan, like white and black pieces on a chessboard, are at war over whose world system shall rule creation" (p. 92). To those trapped on the losing side, Denzel Washington's character in *The Equalizer* offers a piece of wisdom—"Change Your World," which I adopted as the title of Chapter 9. I could as easily have also used this as the title of this book. Changing worlds, rather than changing "the world," is foundational to embodying God.

In "Waybread of Elves," Chapter 10, we'll see that God the "Father's" language is way more wild, controversial, profoundly mystical, and outright outrageous than mortal minds can handle. Thus, to hear and learn from the Father we must first eat what Tolkien calls *lembas*, the waybread of Elves" (p. 95). Embodying God is wild because God is wild, which requires us to cultivate our immortal capacity to exercise a mythological consciousness, that is, a mystical imagination. Perhaps you'll conclude otherwise, but I think some of the most outrageous statements in this book lurk in this chapter. Have fun.

I love Chapter 11, "Circle Me, Lord," because it deals with a form of prayer—encircling prayer—that is as natural as breathing and is one of the most potent practices in establishing colonies of heaven on earth that embody God. "'Circle me, Lord.' The First Adam didn't pray this way nor invite his wife to join him in such a prayer. However, the Second Adam does pray this way and invites His bride, the Church, to join Him in praying this way too" (pp. 104-105).

Embodying God

As I say in the opening of Chapter 12, "Jane Austen Rules!" "When left to my own devices I tend to indulge in Star Trekish type stories. But alas, I'm married to a Jane Austen enthusiast" (p. 108). A thread of nobility, heroism, and chivalry runs deep through Jane Austen's stories, qualities vital to the quest of embodying God in colonies of heaven on earth.

In Chapter 13, "A Colony of Heaven," Sheila's great-grandfather, Johannes Wolff, Jr. helps us "see that heavenly citizenship isn't just for heaven anymore" (p. 116). On July 25, 1889, Johannes signed a document in his quest to become a citizen of the United States that illustrates brilliantly how the "Church on earth is a colony of heaven's citizens commissioned to heavenize earth" (p. 113).

On a scale from one to ten, with ten being the highest, "What's Your Value?" Chapter 14 explores this question as we follow Presbyter Tim Abel's work of "forming a colony of heaven on earth by giving people a place to belong to believe instead of requiring them to believe before they can belong" (p. 117). As Tim models in his life coaching, a genuine colony of heaven is a place where people experience healing, get discipled and belong, even before they believe.

Who's going to populate these colonies of heaven on earth? The answer may surprise you as we'll see in Chapter 15, "Something Big's Happening." At times we may feel that evil is so powerful that forming a community to embody God is a fool's errand. But human beings have a limited capacity to kick against their destiny. They eventually weary of resisting and get on board with God's wonderful plan for their lives. "Forbidden fruit never satisfies. The more we eat, the

Introduction

hungrier we get" (p. 127). Prodigals all in good time come to their senses and come home. Then we celebrate.

It's back to the movies—four of them in "Dangerous Paths Taken," Chapter 16. One of the most gripping parts of any story is the "point where the hero and his or her friends make a costly choice. Contrary to the instinct for self-preservation, they take dangerous paths into the heart of darkness to destroy evil and save the world" (p. 129). The determination of heroes to take dangerous paths transforms colonies of hell on earth into colonies of heaven on earth.

With Chapter 17, "Faith in Humanity," we bring these meditations to a close by contemplating this: "Having faith in God doesn't magically make the world a better place. Having God's faith in humanity does" (p. 132). Embodying God in colonies of heaven on earth is destined for success precisely because divine-human union is God's idea, not ours. That is somehow comforting.

In the Afterword, I pick up and bring to conclusion some of my ponderings introduced in the Preface.

In overview, each chapter herein is a creative, imaginative exploration of but a few of the times and places in life where humanity and divinity intersect. As such, each meditation serves as a kind of rest stop along the way where we can pause and marvel at the peculiarities, dangers, and wonders of embodying God in colonies of heaven on earth.

1

EMBODYING GOD

Fifteenth Week after Pentecost, 2015

MY APPROACHING CONSECRATION as an Abbot Bishop on Saturday, January 9, 2016 has got me pondering. What is the Lord calling me to do in this next season of life, here on planet earth?

So, in the safety of the secret counsel of many, I would like to share with you a pilgrim's roadmap that I find myself compelled to follow. This roadmap, however, isn't just for my journey alone. I hope and expect, since you're reading this, that your pilgrimage and mine will overlap in increasingly exciting ways. After all, ultimately, none of us travels alone, although it may feel that way at times because we often get separated from one another on the road.

All of us have a glorious *individual* destiny and also a *collective*, shared one, culminating in an outrageous wee little thing called *embodying God*. We're each divinely crafted by God in the image of God as *icons of God*. But a dragon darkness has crept into the world, obscuring this glorious truth, trying to keep Mankind pinned down in the dust. Thus, the journey, the struggle, and the hope.

As I wrote in *Epic Living*, evil's best attempts to disfigure us shall not ultimately succeed in depriving us of the victory and joy of embodying God.

LEPERS EMBODYING GOD

Disfigured by the darkness that has crept into the world, I've become a leper in need of healing. Truth be told, we're all lepers, and the Church is a colony of lepers in need of healing.

As Saint Gregory says,

> There lies before our eyes a dreadful and pathetic sight...human beings alive yet dead, disfigured in almost every part of their bodies, barely recognizable for who they once were or where they came from...even the most kind and considerate person shows no feeling for them...we actually believe that avoiding these people assures the safety of our own bodies.

Saint Gregory pretty well sums up my experience over the years of living with myself and others, and especially others in the Church. Though we are a disfigured lot, we remain icons of God. How can this be? The light of *Christus Victor's* Incarnation overcomes the darkness. Thus your destiny and mine, the destiny of every person, and also that of the Church, is not to waste away to nothing, but to be restored to embody God *in our flesh*.

Lepers embodying God? Outrageous? Totally, which makes this the great story of the ages, a pilgrim's story fueled by the Father's passion for the restoration of all things, a hero's journey fraught with challenge and peril. There will be adventures, dangerous ones, and in the midst of them, great joy.

CARE FOR THE BODY

Saint Gregory goes on to make a wonderful observation about his own body.

> How I came to be joined to it, I do not know; nor how I am the image of God and concocted of clay at the same time; this body...that I both cherish as a fellow-servant and evade as my enemy...If I struggle to suppress it, I lose the helper I need to achieve my noble aims, knowing that it is through my actions that I am to ascend to God.

Saint Gregory concludes, "We must, my brothers [*and sisters*]...care for the body as being our kinsman and fellow-servant."

True, authentic faith deals with "the things needed for the body" (James 2:16). As portrayed in the Icon of the Resurrection, the body must be raised out of Hades. So, how do I see myself called in this next season to care for my body, the bodies of others, and the Body of Christ? In five ways.

PLANTING "LOCAL CHURCHES" FIFTH

The last thing, that is, the *fifth* thing I intend to set my hand to do with Basileia is plant what some people call "local churches." Four other priorities come first. However, together *all five* of these priorities form a whole greater than the sum of the parts—a *covenantal* whole that unites individuals in the Capital C Church to embody God *on earth*.

Embodying God

These five priorities are:

1. Start Abbeys
2. Commission Eucharistic Servers
3. Release Initiatives
4. Multiply Chapters
5. Form Fellowships

After I first share the story of how I discovered these five priorities—which I think of as five milestones of the journey—-I'll then define what each one means.

CELTIC COLONIES OF HEAVEN

Fifteen years ago I learned that the ancient Celtic Church didn't plant "local churches," but built colonies of heaven. From the fifth through the eighth centuries, the Celts formed over one thousand of these heavenizing-earth outposts. The first ones appeared in Ireland, followed by others to the east at Iona and Lindisfarne, and then hundreds more sprung up across northern Europe. As Thomas Cahill puts it, following the collapse of the Roman Empire, these colonies "saved civilization."

We've come full circle. The Winter season has come *again*. Many modern empires are in a state of collapse, affording us the opportunity to let go of the old and embrace the new. Thus, to greet the coming Spring with wisdom, power, and strength in our bones, now is the time to embrace a twenty-first-century approach to forming colonies of heaven.

Embodying God

We can learn a lot from the ancient Celtic Christian settlements that rose as Rome fell. These colonies functioned as the heart of the Kingdom on earth. Embodying God was their overall, unifying vision. Each community was typically laid out in a circle, large enough to encompass hundreds, even thousands of people and animals. In the middle was an Abbey. Around the perimeter of the community was a three foot high circular stone wall, marking where the Fallen World System ended and the Kingdom of God began. To enter the community was to *cross over into another world*. Imagine oak trees planted just inside the wall, creating a ring of trees around the entire community. Under these oaks various guilds or vocational groups gathered—artisans, educators, blacksmiths, farmers, and others. Each practiced a very earthy sort of praying throughout the day. The blacksmiths had special prayers for lighting fires, just as the farmers had their prayers for milking cows. Such Celtic daily prayer was at the heart of a lifestyle of embodying God in every moment, in every task, in every breath, in every person. Between the Abbey and the oak trees were clearings for guest houses and other meeting places for fellowship and sharing life.

In *The Fellowship of the Ring*, Tolkien fancifully captures the dynamic of these Celtic colonies in epic descriptions of Lothlórien, "the heart of elvendom on earth." As Frodo experienced it, upon arriving in Lothlórien,

> "It seemed to him that he had stepped over a bridge of time into a corner of the Elder Days, and was now walking in a world that was no more. In Rivendell there was memory of ancient things; in Lórien the ancient things still lived on in the waking world."

The vision of thin place communities, where the veil between heaven and earth is wispy thin, has captured my imagination.

Embodying God in the Abbey, Under the Oak Tree, and Everywhere in-Between

I and my fellow Basileians have conducted fifteen years of research and development on this Celtic-inspired way of doing Church. We've built prototypes, not out of a nostalgic yearning to recreate a Celtic past, but with future-ancient eyes fixed on the Kingdom's future. Now it's time to *multiply* communities of the Church that operate as thin place colonies, embassies, outposts of heaven on earth, dedicated to embodying God in all areas of thought and life. I see this unfolding in five stages:

1. Start Abbeys

In our twenty-first-century basileian way of doing things an Abbey is an apostolic team called to build a Basileia Community. For example, I presently serve as the Presiding Abbot of the Abbey of St. John, based in Colorado Springs. Our Abbey is an apostolic team engaged in building the Basileia Community of St. John, a colony of heaven on earth. Here in the twenty-first century, our members also include those spread out across the globe, whom we connect with virtually.

Our Abbeys are like mustard seeds that give rise to mustard trees, i.e., to entire communities. Therefore, the highest priority of an apostolic team is to assemble in Sunday Eucharistic worship shaped by the rhythm of the Church Year where we are healed of our leprosy and restored as icons of God. Facing and owning the poverty of our fallen human condition is the first and necessary step in our journey of *theosis* (deification)—of our participation in the life of the Trinity, which makes us partakers of the divine nature.

Once we plug into God via the Divine Liturgy, then we extend His divine life outward, first by commissioning Eucharistic Servers.

2. Commission Eucharistic Servers

In Chapter 2, "The Empire of God," I tell the story in detail of how worshipers in the early centuries brought small loaves of bread with them to Eucharistic worship services. While one main loaf was broken and eaten during the service, these small loaves were not, even though the Bishop consecrated these loaves during the service. Instead, each worshiper took his or her little loaf with them to share with others throughout the week who were not at the service. This extended approach to celebrating the Eucharist served as a powerful, practical, and tangible way of giving expression to the organic unity of the Body of Christ in every corner of daily life.

Sharing consecrated bread with people not at a liturgical Eucharistic service is not a substitute for assembling as the Church, but rather *another way* of assembling as the Church. Extending communion to those who for whatever reason can't or won't yet come to a corporate Eucharistic worship service is a way to bodily and tangibly demonstrate that the Church is bigger than any one particular expression. Commissioning Eucharistic Servers is a kind of inverse Trojan Horse strategy.

Thus, it is my joyful ambition to see our Abbey train and commission dozens, even hundreds, of Eucharistic Servers. We will multiply Servers to share consecrated bread back in their homes, businesses, apartment complexes, under bridges with the homeless, in prisons, and even in space. Yes, in *space*, just like what Buzz Aldrin did on July 20, 1969. Immediately after landing on the moon, Aldrin celebrated communion with bread and wine that his pastor gave him back on earth. Now, that's what I'm talking about!

A network of people sharing communion together throughout the community, not only on Sundays in the Abbey but also Monday through Saturday beyond the Abbey, better positions us to release Initiatives.

3. RELEASE INITIATIVES

Initiatives take place "under the oak tree," at the edges of the community. In 2014, Sheila and I started an Initiative called *CenterPoint*, which functions as a basileian cottage industry in the area of business, wealth creation, and personal finance. Basileian educators, Presbyter Fraser Haug and Deaconess Puanana Haug, have started *Montessori schools*. Dan and Faye Smithwick founded a worldview Institute named *Nehemiah*. Presbyter Tim Abel in Wales has founded *Transformations*, a life coaching Initiative ripe for multiplication around the world. Presbyter John Hunt and I have launched *Kingdom Superheroes*, "a global community of chivalric adventurers engaged in an epic lifestyle of heroically advancing the Kingdom of Christ."

Initiatives mainly provide kingdom hospitality and services to *guests*, i.e., people who are not necessarily believers or even members of the community. We see such guests as *icons of God*, lepers like ourselves destined for transformation by the Grace of God.

Hosting Initiatives is hard because we must confront and overcome the temptation to *stigmatize* others just because they have leprosy (as if we don't). We must resist the temptation of "avoiding these people," as Saint Gregory says, to assure "the safety of our own bodies." We cannot allow ourselves to be overwhelmed by fear of being overcome by the leprous conditions of others and then use that fear as an excuse to avoid facing our own leprous condition. The autonomous traditions of men justify all forms of stigmatization—racism, sexism, denominationalism—by concluding that "lepers" deserve their fate, being cursed by God. Our unfounded but real fears of being abandoned by God fuel these views—views from the pit.

Eucharistic worship is the fundamental way we embrace the path of *kenosis* and deal with our fear of being abandoned by God. Thus, we root and anchor all of our Initiatives deep in the life of the Church through what we call Chapters of Vocational Societies.

4. MULTIPLY CHAPTERS

Regardless of the terminology used, every civilization naturally forms "chapters" or "associations" for every conceivable vocational area of thought and life. Modern societies, for example, have associations for educators, scientists, realtors, travel, chicken farmers, skydivers, chess players, dogs owners, cat owners, fashion, and so on. A comprehensive list would contain thousands of different types of associations.

CenterPoint, for example, is an Initiative of the Abbey of St. John Entrepreneurs, a Chapter that is both membered to our Society of Entrepreneurs and our Abbey. What we call "Chapters" are how we use associations for building colonies of heaven.

Our Basileian Chapters are *vocational* expressions of kingdom civilization, rooted in the Church. Chapters enable us to identify, train and commission people via the laying on of hands as *ministers* in their particular vocational areas of life. The very word "vocation" means a "calling" from God. Being ordained as an officer in the Church is but one diaconal path of service in the Kingdom among many. Each path is of equal value though different in function. Our Chapters affirm the nobility and unique genius of all vocational areas and make it public, giving us yet another way of embodying God.

Chapters form somewhere between the Abbey and the Oak Tree, which is also the case with Fellowships.

5. FORM FELLOWSHIPS

A "Fellowship" is simply the term we use for what some call a "local church," or what classical churches call a "parish."

Forming Fellowships is the fifth milestone on the journey. I place this milestone fifth because many today lug around heavy baggage in their perceptions of and experiences with the "local church." By first 1) starting Abbeys, 2) commissioning Eucharistic Servers, 3) releasing Initiatives, and 4) multiplying Chapters, much of this baggage can be cut away. Fellowships that emerge organically out of a community dedicated to these first four milestones enables both unbelievers and believers to freshly discover the Church as an Ecclesial City.

Putting Fellowships fifth paves the way for unbelievers to discover the Church as a "belong to believe" community of God versus a "believe to belong" institution captive to the traditions of men. And putting Fellowships fifth gives believers an opportunity to detox from bad past "church" experiences so that they might then rediscover the Church in a fresh, organic, and relational way.

Who can say what form Fellowships may take as we move further into the twenty-first century. Whatever their form, they are yet another vital way of embodying God in a colony of heaven, which for Fellowships means embodying God somewhere in-between the Abbey and the Oak Tree.

Conclusion

Saint John Chrysostom says that we may see,

> Christ's Body…lying everywhere, in the alleys and in the market places, and you may sacrifice upon it [as you would an altar] anytime…When then you see a poor believer, believe that you are beholding an altar. When you see this one as a beggar, do not only refrain from insulting him, but actually give him honor, and if you witness someone else insulting him, stop him; prevent it.

Humanity is an altar made holy by the Incarnation. Evil doesn't ultimately shape our destiny; the goodness of God does. Thus, giving ourselves to the epic quest of embodying

Embodying God

God in our leprous bodies is how we exhaust evil. Even as our bodies are being healed, forming colonies of heaven is the surest way to cut the legs out from under all the sophisticated relational and institutional nonsense of the traditions of men. Forgetting that we're all lepers only encourages the traditions "of this world"—versus those "from above"—to shun others as lepers, which tragically spiritualizes and sentimentalizes the Faith into irrelevancy.

Let's get relevant.

Embodying God on earth as lepers who are on the mend doesn't deny heaven, but embraces and honors heaven as the pattern for earth. Our missional objective is to *heavenize earth* by replacing the Fallen World System with the Kingdom of God. Thus embracing lepers everywhere is an inevitable, good, and necessary thing, beginning with the one who stares back at us in the mirror. Every person remains an icon of God no matter how deeply the power of evil twists them. Therefore, no person is ultimately able to resist their own untwisting, for by Grace we are restored to our common call and destiny of embodying God, even if we kick against the goads. Embodying God is an inevitability planted deep in our bones. Such a view of things compels me all the more to follow the pilgrim's roadmap given to me with abandon—this map with its five milestones.

We fight *from* victory, not for it.

I look forward to making this journey with you in all the wild ways that are no doubt in store for us just ahead as well as over the not so distant horizon.

2

THE EMPIRE OF GOD

Second Week after Pentecost, 2015

THE ROMAN EMPIRE DIDN'T have a problem with Christian believers, but with Christian *worshipers*.

While all worshipers are believers, not all believers are worshipers. When Rome caught a Christian worshiper in the act, Rome first tried to turn the worshiper back into a mere believer. But if the worshiper stood fast, he or she was put to death before sunset.

The Christian worship services Rome feared were typically over in twenty minutes and lacked music to stir the emotions or sermons to gird the mind. While the nature of these services may be a mystery to many of us modern Christians, Rome knew they were a supreme threat to the Empire. What did Rome know?

Rome knew a lot about worship. Roman Emperors were the *lead* worshipers of the Empire. The Caesars of Rome, no less the Pharaohs of Egypt, weren't just kings. They were also *priests*. Rome's priest-kings regularly officiated over pagan worship services—services with no music or sermons. These services made the Roman Empire the Roman Empire. To understand this is to understand worship.

Worshipers establish empires. While armies are good for *defending* an empire against all enemies foreign and domestic, armies don't *build* empires. Worshipers do. Liturgical and ceremonial acts of priest-kings build and sustain empires. Only after the priest-kings have done their job do believers have a place to call home.

THE ROAD TO TREASON

Imagine you're a Christian within the Roman Empire some time in the first three centuries of the Christian era. It's 4:30 am on Sunday morning. You're getting ready for work because, during these centuries, Sunday is a workday. You slip a miniature loaf of bread in your pocket as you leave home. This bread isn't for lunch, but for a special secret counsel meeting you're participating in before work, one held every Sunday morning.

You head to a neighborhood with a large home owned by a wealthy Christian family. Looking over your shoulder to be sure no one is following, you quietly make your way to the backside of the house and slip in the backdoor. A man guarding the door, a Deacon, checks you out to be sure you're one of the regulars. He recognizes you, smiles and waves you in.

In the large central room, a couple dozen people have already gathered. You know most of them. At the far end of the room sits an older, stately, bearded man, the Bishop. Two

Deacons stand to his left and right. They occasionally bend down to say something to him. In the middle is a semicircle of chairs for the Presbyters, who have already taken their seats.

The Traitors Assemble

The Bishop stands and greets the room saying, "The Lord be with you." In unison all respond, "And also with you." At once there is silence and order. In front of the Bishop is a waist-high table. You and the rest of the worshipers pack into the space before the Bishop flanked by the Deacons within the semicircle bounded by the Presbyters. Now the Church is assembled. Now the meeting begins—this meeting for liturgical Eucharistic worship. You won't be there more than twenty minutes. It wouldn't be wise. After all, as far as Rome is concerned, you're committing treason.

Everyone turns to one another, extends a blessing, saying, "The peace of Christ." The two Deacons flanking the Bishop spread a white tablecloth on the table. One of the Deacons holds out a plate, signaling everyone to file forward to offer their small loaves. The Deacon sets the plate on the table and the Bishop adds his own small loaf to the pile. The other Deacon adds a little water to a cup of wine. All stand in silence.

The Presbyters stretch out their hands toward the table. The Bishop stretches his hands over the table and begins a dialogue form of prayer with the worshipers. After the initial dialogue, the Bishop prays another five minutes in the Holy Spirit, thanking the Father for the work of Christ. When the Bishop finishes, in unison all say, "Amen."

COMMITTING A CAPITAL OFFENSE

The Bishop takes and breaks one of the loaves, then tears off a piece and eats it. He takes a sip from the cup. The Deacons break the loaf into enough pieces for everyone. You and the rest of the worshipers file up to the table to receive a piece. The Bishop places it into your hands saying, "The Bread of Heaven in Jesus Christ." You respond, "Amen." One of the Deacons then offers you a sip from the cup, saying, "In God the Father Almighty and in the Lord Jesus Christ and in the Holy Spirit in the Holy Church." You respond, "Amen."

After everyone has filed back to their spot, all pause for a moment of silence. Then, for the third and final time during this secret counsel meeting, everyone files back to the table to receive one of the small loafs from the plate. You'll take this home and celebrate communion with your family later that day after work, that is if you get home.

As you take your loaf, you remember your friend John, who was spotted, arrested, and executed a few months ago after attending one of these liturgical Eucharistic worship gatherings. You say a prayer for John's widow and three kids.

"CHRISTIANS! CHRISTIANS!"

After the distribution of the loaves, the Deacons clean the plate and cup. One of the Deacons pronounces a blessing and commissions all to go in the joy of the Lord. If this is like most Sundays, then over the next ten or fifteen minutes everyone will file out the back door individually or in pairs and quietly slip out of the neighborhood. Doing it this way helps prevent some neighbor from becoming alarmed that Christians have gathered in the neighborhood and alert the authorities.

But this Sunday is not destined to be like most. From out in front of the house comes a shout, "Christians! Christians!" Within moments, windows and doors fly open up and down the street. A crowd gathers. The crowd becomes a mob.

The Bishop, flanked by the two Deacons, comes out on the front steps as shouts of "Christians! Christians!" continue to erupt from the crowd. The first soldier arrives, looks at the Bishop and demands, "What is this? Are you a Christian?" "Yes I am," replies the Bishop. Someone in the crowd blurts out, "They're all Christians!" More soldiers arrive. You're among ten people still in the house with no way out. You're all arrested for committing the capital crime of Christian Eucharistic worship. You have challenged the authority of the Emperor and now will face the consequences. You're bound and hauled before the local Roman magistrate where "justice" will be served that day.

GUILTY OR NOT GUILTY?

The soldiers escort you and the others into a stark room. On one side sits the magistrate in front of a table. On the opposite side of the room is an imposing statue of the deified Emperor. In front of the statue is a small bowl of incense next to a burning, brazen altar.

One by one, soldiers bring your friends before the magistrate. He asks each one a simple question, "Do you plead guilty or not guilty?" If you answer, "Guilty," then your fate is sealed.

But at the critical moment some falter, blurting out, "Not guilty." Immediately, these are grabbed by the arm and hauled in front of the statue of the Emperor. A test of their confession is required. They must take a pinch of incense, toss it on the brazen altar and declare, "Caesar is Lord." Do this and you're free. But if you do, from this day forward you will be excommunicated from the Table of the Lord, remaining a believer, but not a worshiper.

Now it's your turn to face the magistrate. What will you do?

The magistrate asks the group of the guilty if any more would like to repent and burn incense to the Emperor before judgment is passed. All stand firm. You are among worshipers now, not just believers. The penalty is death. There is no appeal. The law is final: *non licet esse chrstianos* ("Christians may not exist"). There is no delay. The sentence is carried out that day.

WHICH EMPIRE?

Not by power or by might, but in the secret counsel meeting of the *ecclesia* where the Spirit makes the bread and wine for us the body and blood of Christ—this is how the Empire of God is built. Every empire is built by such acts of worship. Just ask Caesar.

All believers are members of some empire. The only question is which empire.

Do we think that the Kingdom of God is merely some belief system? No. The kingdom of God is way more dangerous than that. The Kingdom of God is a *world* system. It is the Empire of God.

Have we so sentimentalized and sanitized Jesus' title, "King of kings and Lord of lords," that it escapes us that this is the title of an Emperor?

Let's give believers everywhere a home in the Empire of God. Let's worship!

3

THE POLITICS OF WORSHIP

Fourth Week After Pentecost, 2015

TO UNDERSTAND WORSHIP is to understand politics.

One of my favorite twentieth-century stories of the inseparable link between worship and politics is that of Karol Wojtyla, who took on the might and folly of the Soviet Empire with bread and wine.

On December 24, 1959, Wojtyla drove a definitive nail in the coffin of Soviet Communism. He did it via a secret counsel gathering for Eucharistic worship in an empty field of Nowa Huta, on the outskirts of Kraków, Poland. This worship service was the moment when the Soviet Union's fall became inevitable. Wojtyla's longtime secretary would write years after the Christmas Eve Eucharist service of 1959, that it "began right there in Nowa Huta."

Embodying God

NOWA HUTA

In 1949, the communist occupiers of Poland came up with the "brilliant" idea to create the first Polish city with no church. It was the biggest mistake the communists ever made.

They envisioned a model socialist city, a proletarian paradise of Stalinist propaganda. They named it Nowa Huta, meaning "New Steelworks."

Not only did the communists intend for Nowa Huta to have no church, but socialist urban planners created apartment complexes housing 40,000 workers with modules designed to keep people separated from each other. To visit a neighbor required taking the stairs or the elevator to the ground floor, exiting the building, then re-entering the building through a different doorway. People then had to locate and ascend the unique set of stairs or elevator that went to their neighbor's housing module. Any form of community loyalty other than to the state was forbidden.

But the workers of Nowa Huta and Karol Wojtyla saw things differently.

WOJTYLA GOES HEAD ON WITH THE COMMUNISTS

On July 4, 1958, Wojtyla was appointed the auxiliary bishop of Kraków. On Christmas Eve, 1959, Wojtyla chose an open field in the Bienczyce neighborhood of Nowa Huta to make his stand against the Soviet Empire. He led hundreds of workers to erect a large cross and then set up the Table for a Eucharistic worship service.

The Politics of Worship

As portrayed in a 2005 cinematic recreation of the scene, the worshipers were surrounded by soldiers. But Wojtyla simply announced that Christ already had a house in Nowa Huta. This house was His Church that Christ had established in Poland a millennium before the communists arrived and that would be there long after the communists left. In the film, some soldiers remove their helmets and cross themselves.

The central purpose of Christian Eucharistic worship is to concretely and publically witness to the fact that Christ in His Church is alive and well on planet earth. There's nothing any army, or politician, or human empire can do about it. What's done is done. He's here.

THE COMMUNISTS IMPLODE

Unable to derail Wojtyla's Christmas Eve Eucharistic worship service, the communists pulled down the cross from the open field on April 27, 1960, sparking a riot.

Desperate to regain control of the city, the communist politicians prevailed upon Wojtyla to write a letter to the townspeople, instructing them to refrain from further violence and protests. But Wojtyla outwitted the politicians by writing a letter to the people declaring there was no reason for further protests since in the future the people would set up the cross again, and the communists would not remove it.

The political authorities predictably rejected Wojtyla's letter. So Wojtyla responded by raising the stakes even further. He proposed adding a statement to the letter that the only way to keep the peace in Nowa Huta would be for the people to build a church, not just erect a cross.

As portrayed in the 2005 film, the communists wrongly thought that because Wojtyla was a "dreamer" and a "poet," that he was "fundamentally benign." They imagined him as someone "open to persuasion," who could be "manipulated and controlled." But poetry, especially the poetry of grace enacted in the Liturgy, is the language of heroes, not elegiac pessimists. Confidence that Christ is building His Church and that the gates of Hades will not prevail is something for which communists have no category. This makes them irrelevant and subject to extinction.

BUILDING THE ARK

Wojtyla and the workers of Nowa Huta continued to assemble in the open field each Christmas Eve for the next two decades.

In a vain attempt to keep control of the situation, the communists finally issued a building permit for a church on October 13, 1967. The next day, Wojtyla went to the open field with a pickaxe to help dig the first section of the church's foundation.

In 1969, Wojtyla laid the first cornerstone of the church—a rock from the Apostle Peter's grave in Rome.

Over the next several years, the communists revoked the building permit, confiscated building materials and appropriated (i.e., stole) donations. On August 15, 1976, Nowa Huta's local priest, Józef Kurzeja, after enduring constant police harassment and interrogations, died of a heart attack at age 40. Nevertheless, people from all over Poland collected two million polished stones from Poland's rivers to decorate the outside of the church. Volunteer laborers from Poland and Europe pieced the structure together brick by brick.

On May 15, 1977, the church structure was completed and named, Arka Pana, "The Lord's Ark." Through His Church, Christ transports people in an ark from a lost and ruined world to a new and lasting one. Built in the modernist style of Swiss architect Le Corbusier, Arka Pana is shaped like Noah's Ark to symbolize the Polish Church's triumph over godless communism.

People attended the dedication ceremony from across Poland and Europe. They came from Yugoslavia, Czechoslovakia, and Hungary. East Germans showed up from the German Democratic Republic. Others came from Western Germany and Austria. A Dutch delegation came to hear the bells they had donated. Other delegations came from France, Belgium, Portugal, Great Britain, the United States, Finland, and Italy. One guest came from Japan. A moon rock collected by Apollo 11 and given to Pope Paul VI ended up in the center of the church's tabernacle—a tabernacle sculpted to symbolize the cosmos.

In an oxymoronic twist, the steelworkers of Nowa Huta cranked up the Lenin Steelworks to create a gigantic figure of Christ.

At the dedication, Wojtyla declared,

> "This is not a city of people...who may be manipulated according to the laws or rules of production and consumption. This is a city of the children of God [and] this temple was needed so that this could be expressed, [so] that it could be emphasized..."

Embodying God

Then, just over a year later, on October 22, 1978, Karol Wojtyla was elected to be the Bishop of Rome, a job most people recognize as that of Pope. Wojtyla took the name John Paul II. Communist politicians the world over could be heard collectively uttering a deep sigh that this "dreamer," this "poet" was now positioned to finish what he had started in Nowa Huta.

THE COLLAPSE OF THE SOVIET EMPIRE

The dedication ceremony of the Lord's Ark was a global testimony to communist totalitarianism's failure and the triumph of Christ and His Church.

Eight months after being elected Bishop of Rome, John Paul II visited his homeland of Poland, arriving on June 2, 1979, during one of the early weeks of the Church Year following Pentecost.

John Paul II directly challenged the communist government, but not by leading an uprising. He simply did in 1979 what he had done in Nowa Huta in 1959. He broke out the bread and wine.

There's nothing magical about bread and wine in Eucharistic worship, but there is something sacramental. The bread and wine testify to an *accomplished fact*, namely that the kingdoms of this world have become the kingdoms of our Lord and of His Christ. In short, Christ is *already* here and there's nothing politicians can do about it except bow the knee.

On Sunday, June 10, 1979, John Paul II led a Eucharistic worship service in the Blonie Field of Kraków. It was the largest gathering of humanity in Poland's history. Two million or three million or more came to this secret counsel gathering and experienced the certainty of Christ's presence among them. This certainty afterward spread and galvanized the courage of ten million in Poland, bringing communism in Poland to an end. Then, what happened in Poland spread over Eastern Europe, catalyzing the collapse of communism in one country after another. The Soviet Union dissolved on December 26, 1991.

On the night before Christmas in 1959, true to the Christmas story itself, the communists had no place for Christ in their socialist Inn. On the day after Christmas in 1991, the communists were ushered out of Christ's house into the footnotes of history.

History belongs to *worshipers* of Emperor Jesus. You can't get more political than that.

4

THE PHYSICS OF SPIRITUALITY

Fourth Sunday of Pascha (Easter), 2015

As I learned from my Italian Grandpa and Grandma, good meals begin with bread and wine.

I remember an especially memorable meal Grandpa and Grandma hosted for one of my occasional visits during my college days. Gathered that night were an assortment of aunts and uncles, cousins and guests. As the evening progressed, the conversation came around to how my studies were going. I laughed that my college career had recently averted shipwreck. "To graduate," I said, "I have to take both Genetics and Old Testament History. But the college had scheduled both classes at the same time. Thankfully, after pleading for my academic life, the college rescheduled the Genetics class, paving my way to graduation glory."

BIOLOGY AND THE BIBLE

One of the guests asked, "What kind of major requires taking classes like that?" "Well," I explained, "I'm double majoring in biology and Bible." This guest then put down her fork, stared at me in utter bewilderment and asked, "But how do you deal with the *internal conflict?*"

Grandma sent the bowl of spaghetti around the table again as I responded, "Well, not only are the Scriptures divinely authored, but Jesus is also the 'author of life.' So, I'm on a quest to read everything God has written, not only in Scripture, but also in that amazing story inscribed into the DNA molecules of all living things."

It's an unusual thing when a table of Italians fall silent. But I testify truly that such a miracle happened that night if just for the briefest of moments. *Everyone* at this point put down their forks and fixed their eyes upon me to see what would happen next.

Word Made Flesh

Being fuller of myself than I was of Grandma's spaghetti, I opened my mouth yet again and waxed on. "You see, my major in biblical studies deals with the 'Word of God' and my biology major deals with 'flesh.' There's a verse in the Bible that says, 'The Word became flesh,' So, doing these two majors enables me to explore this mystery from both sides at the same time. Doesn't the idea of Word becoming flesh suggest there's an *inherent unity* of the physical and the spiritual instead of an internal conflict?"

As the silence deepened even more, Grandpa broke it with a question of his own: "More wine anyone?"

THE BODY OF CHRIST

As I've continued to ponder the physics of the spirituality of Word made flesh over the years, the mystery has deepened. I'm especially blown away these days by the fact there are three distinct things called "The Body of Christ." There is 1) Christ's physical body in which Word became flesh in the Incarnation and then was raised in the Resurrection, 2) the Church and 3) the bread and wine of the Lord's Supper.

Western Christian thinking emphasizes the *distinctions* between similar things while Eastern Christian thinking emphasizes the *similarities* between distinct things. It's true that Christ's physical body, the Church and the bread and wine of the Lord's Supper are all distinct. Nevertheless, they are, in fact, each more the same than different. Together, these three are *Totus Christus*, the "Total Christ," head, body, bread and blood as one.

EMBODIED SPIRITUALITY

The divine-human dialog around the Lord's Table, just like Grandpa and Grandma modeled, starts with bread and wine.

The physics of resurrection flesh is not something to reason toward, but from. What does resurrected flesh look like and do? Prayerfully imagine yourself sitting with Christ at His Table, eating bread and drinking wine with your fellow "kings and priests" with whom you "reign on the earth." Now that's a supper!

More significant than the next session of Congress or the next act of Parliament is the gathering of Christ and His

Church for the resurrection meal called the Lord's Supper. This meal is where, in secret counsel, writers script the course of space and time. It's all written here, everything from Scripture to DNA molecules.

It may seem counterintuitive at first, but if your spiritual life has stagnated, then pinch your flesh to find the way forward again. Nothing cures dullness of spirit better than a good reminder that it is via flesh that the Word came to dwell among His ruined creation. He then died and was resurrected into an immortal state beyond death's reach forevermore.

THE END OF MARXISM, FREUDIANISM AND DARWINISM

Spiritualistic and materialistic notions of the world are scandalous. They both suffer from an underdeveloped sense of the Resurrection as an accomplished fact. The image of God in us isn't just a "spiritual" reality, but also one for the physics books. And there's more to physics than just "physics." Failure to make the Resurrection as much about physics as it is about invisible "spiritual" things opens the gate to the likes of Marxism, Freudianism, and Darwinism.

The undoing of Marxism begins the moment we recognize that man is not merely a material being who lives on bread alone. *Totus Christus* testifies that man lives according to every word that proceeds from the mouth of God. Chew on that! Fasting from the Tree of the Knowledge of Good and Evil as Jesus did during His forty day fast demonstrates that there is something more fundamental to the nature of our humanity than the need for food.

Embodying God

Who needs Freudian psychology when the resurrection state, rather than sex, holds the key to the true nature of human existence. Freudianism presupposes that sex is a more fundamental defining factor of humanity than religion, when in fact it is the Resurrection that shapes religion. Resurrected flesh speaks to the true nature of Mankind created as an immortal being who does not require the institution of marriage in the resurrection state to navigate eternity.

And who needs Darwinism when the physics of the Resurrection transforms us from a mortal state to an immortal, superhuman state? Darwinism is a school of thought that modern minds fell prey to because we know in the deepest parts of our souls that transformative glory, not the lowly mortal state of the Fall, is our destiny. Darwinism is a problem for which the Resurrection flesh of *Totus Christus* is the solution.

More wine anyone?

5

GAME ON!

Feast of Pentecost, 2015

A FEW YEARS AGO I HAD a Pentecostal religious experience, but not in a church. It happened in a sports temple.

While on a business trip to San Francisco with Rick Barry, one of the fifty greatest basketball players in the game's history, I witnessed something divine. What I saw suggests why so many famous sports trophies are in the form of a cup.

PILGRIMAGE TO THE OLYMPIC CLUB

Our last meeting of the day was hosted downtown at the Olympic Club, a unique facility containing a dining room, meeting rooms, guest rooms, banquet rooms, two pools, and a couple basketball courts.

Upon arriving out front, we ascended the stairs from the street-level realm of mortals into the temple, past tree-sized marble columns, into the outer sanctuary, which some people unimaginatively call "the foyer." Statues of athletic heroes and glass-encased sports memorabilia honoring a pantheon of sports gods and their superhuman accomplishments filled the outer court.

Before our business meeting began, our hosts ushered Rick into one of the inner courts—a basketball court where twenty boys were in the midst of their afternoon practice. The coaches blew their whistles and gathered the boys at Rick's feet to hear from a living, breathing sports legend. After all, those boys weren't there to learn to play basketball but to be coached in the arts of immortality.

Before saying a word, Rick did something extraordinary. His 30.5 points-per-game record with the American Basketball Association still stands as the highest career total for a player in any professional basketball league. His mastery of an unorthodox, but highly accurate underhanded free throw method contributed in no small part to his record. Taking the ball, Rick turned toward the basket, *bowed his head and closed his eyes*, then put the ball through the hoop without looking. Swish!

That got the boys' attention.

THE WINNER'S CUP

Rick's talk aimed to motivate these boys to be the best team players possible, whether in the realm of sports or otherwise. He whet their appetite to taste the thrill of victory and one day hold up the winner's cup in celebration.

Cup-shaped trophies are legion in the sports world. But why?

There's the America's Cup (yacht racing), the Davis Cup (tennis), the Stanley Cup (hockey) and various World Cups for soccer, cricket, alpine skiing, and even chess. There are dozens of more cups, including the Eisenhower Cup (golf), the William's Cup (basketball), and the Swaythling Cup (table tennis). There's the King's Cup (England airplane racing), and the Heineken Cup, one of the most prestigious trophies in Rugby up through 2014.

So what's up with the cup?

Ever hear of that legendary "sporting event" called the quest for the Holy Grail?

Modern sports champions in quest of a cup of victory and the cup of Christ in the Liturgy are the same story. The Arthurian legend links the two.

There's a deep and abiding connection between two types of celebrations that are more the same than different. There are sports champions who celebrate victory by elevating a cup overhead. Then there are priests in the Liturgy who celebrate Christ's victory over all things evil by elevating the cup filled with His blood. Both celebrate the thrill of a victory won by chivalrous heroes who at great sacrifice play by the rules even when others don't.

THE PERILOUS SEAT

What launched the quest for the Holy Grail according to Thomas Malory in *Le Morte d'Arthur* ("The Death of Arthur")? It happened at a secret counsel gathering of King

Arthur's Knights of the Round Table on the Day of Pentecost.

Merlin had reserved a vacant seat at the Round Table, a seat known as the Siege Perilous or the Perilous Seat. It was to remain empty until the arrival of a knight with the purity of heart necessary to succeed in the quest for the Holy Grail. A prophecy foretold that this knight would sit in the Perilous Seat for the first time on the Day of Pentecost.

And then it happened. On Pentecost Sunday in AD 454, the recently knighted Sir Galahad took his place at the Round Table. Being found to be the purest in heart of all knights, he sat in the Perilous Seat. An image of the Holy Grail then appeared floating above the table, a sign to the knights assembled that the time had come to go in search of the Grail. Game on!

In the years that followed, many knights on many adventures sought for the Grail. All ended up badly wounded or worse. Then finally, Sir Galahad, pure in heart and bent only to pursue heavenly ideals, proved indeed to be the greatest of knights, succeeding where others had failed. He obtained the prize, found the Grail and with it, immortality.

THE QUEST IMMORTAL

So yes. Whoever drinks His blood from the cup, Jesus says, "has eternal life" (Jn. 6:54). But are you beginning to see that while the Holy Grail isn't anything less than the cup that Christ lifted up at the Last Supper, it's so much more?

The Holy Grail is also the America's Cup, the Davis Cup, the Stanley Cup and so forth. It is even the Heineken Cup, known in France as the "H Cup" because of the French ban on alcoholic sponsorships.

And yes, it's also true that the legend of King Arthur and his knights is an ancient Celtic-shaped Christian tale. Long before the Celts were introduced to Christ by St. Patrick, they were already dedicated to the making of ceremonial bowls, chalices, and cups. So is it any surprise that the first sports trophies to assume the shape of a cup in the modern era first emerged in the Celtic-shaped lands of the British Isles?

While this is all rather a lot of fun, what's deeply true about it all is that the Holy Grail is the abiding symbol of your quest and mine for *immortality*, regardless of form or approach.

We're all mysteriously drawn to the Quest Immortal. It doesn't matter if you're sailing a boat, smacking a tennis ball, kicking a football, climbing 8,000-meter peaks, playing chess, or drinking Christ's blood from a chalice served by a priest in the Eucharistic worship of the Church. We're all playing the same game for the same prize.

A PENTECOSTAL STORY

The quest for the Holy Grail, whether in ancient legend or modern sports, is at heart a Pentecostal story. Pentecost is the thrill of being made kings and priests who reign on the earth *before* playing the game.

At Pentecost, we're all made new creations in the outpouring of the Spirit. This outpouring is for "all flesh," including "young men," "old men," "male servants," and "female servants" (Acts 2:17-28). Like Galahad, we all may now sit at the Round Table in the Perilous Seat.

Those who sit in the Perilous Seat do not do so because they have already found the Holy Grail. They sit in this sacred place of secret counsel as ones destined to find it.

The greatest champions know the thrill of victory long before ever setting foot on the field of battle. Champions win the cup of victory before the game, not after.

At the Olympic Club that afternoon, Rick made that free throw the instant he bowed his head and closed his eyes. That's why the ball went through the hoop after he released it.

Champions first center down by sitting down in the Perilous Seat and "wait for the promise of the Father" (Acts 1:4). Then it's game on.

6

THE DRUG OF IMMORTALITY

Sixth Week of Pascha (Easter), 2015

I F YOU COULD INGEST A SUBSTANCE that would make you smarter, would you?

We humans have been on a search for a brain-boosting elixir for the mind since the beginning of time. The problem is that most of the substances we've tried along the way have had a nasty side effect called *death*. But there is one substance, one elemental essence alone, whose side effect is godlike knowledge and immortal life.

BAD MEDICINE

Adam and Eve were the first to experiment with a nootropic substance, aka, a "smart drug." They believed that the fruit of the Tree of the Knowledge of Good and Evil could "make one wise," "like God" (Gen. 3:6; v. 5). But what they hoped would be a drug of immortality turned out to be a drug of mortality, killing their hope of better living through chemicals, at least through those particular chemicals.

And so the search for chemical and technological means of intelligence enhancement has continued up to the present day.

Hollywood's Search for Good Medicine

The modern obsession with finding a drug of immortality is on display in movies like *Limitless, Dune, The Matrix,* and *Lucy*.

In *Limitless* (2011 movie), Eddie Morra (Bradley Cooper) finds a solution for writer's bloc—a neuro enhancing drug, NZT-48. After taking one pill, his mental abilities spike and in a flash he's able to complete ninety pages of his stalled book project. He experiments further, using his astonishing new abilities to make a killing in the stock market. But then adverse side effects kick in—blackouts involving huge chunks of time. A year later he's running for the US Senate, with ambitions of becoming President of the United States. Using his new abilities and money, he's tasked the multiple labs he's founded to eliminate the drug's harmful side effects.

In *Dune*, the hero, Paul Atreides (Muad'Dib) drinks the Water of Life, experiencing a transformation that releases superhero-like powers enabling him to complete his messianic mission.

In *The Matrix* (1999 movie), Neo (Keanu Reeves) takes the red pill, catalyzing his transformative journey into a superhero, godlike state in which he eventually defeats the evil Agent Smith and saves the world.

In *Lucy* (2014 movie), Lucy (Scarlett Johansson) is exposed to a drug, CPH4, which kickstarts a transformative process. She

The Drug of Immortality

goes from using only ten percent of her brain capacity to one hundred percent. As Lucy approaches infinite knowledge capacity, she begins to manifest godlike powers of control over space and time. To help her navigate her transfiguration she reaches out to the scientist and doctor, Professor Samuel Norman (Morgan Freeman). The Professor counsels her that the primary purpose of all living things is to pass on the knowledge they've acquired. So at the moment Lucy transitions from a mortal into an immortal state, she finds a way to pass along her newly acquired knowledge of the universe to Professor Norman.

Providentially, only two days *before* watching the movie, *Lucy*, for the first time in my life I encountered the phrase, "the drug of immortality," but not from a Hollywood scriptwriter.

IGNATIUS

While being transported to Rome for his martyrdom by wild beasts nearly two thousand years ago, Ignatius—who the Apostle Peter appointed as the third bishop of Antioch and who was a disciple of the Apostle John—wrote a letter to the Church at Ephesus.

In his characteristically bold and remarkable fashion, Ignatius expressed his view of the sacrament of the Lord's Supper. He spoke of "…breaking one bread, which is the drug of immortality and the antidote that we should not die but live forever in Jesus Christ."

Ignatius' daring language may seem shocking, but that's the nature of the Church (a resurrection community) who celebrates the Lord's Supper (a resurrection meal) on the first day of the week, Sunday (a resurrection day), where every Sunday is a "little Easter."

Ignatius no doubt learned his startling way of speaking of the bread of the Lord's Supper from John, who learned it from Jesus. It was, after all, the Apostle John, who quoted Jesus in his gospel account as saying, "I am the living bread that came down from heaven. If anyone eats of this bread, he will live forever. And the bread that I will give for the life of the world is my flesh" (John 6:51).

What does all this have to do with getting smart? Plenty.

EATING SMART

Scripture speaks of "The Council of the Lord" as a gathering of friends whom the Lord calls together in secret counsel. Gathered at a meal, these friends discuss the meaning of His Word and then enact it as rulers of the world.

I write this in the middle of the Sixth Week of Pascha (Easter) in which the gospel reading on Sunday was from Ignatius' mentor, John, the fifteenth chapter. Around the Table with His disciples at the Last Supper, Jesus said, "No longer do I call you servants, for the servant does not know what his master is doing; but I have called you friends, for all that I have heard from my Father I have made known to you" (v. 15).

What Adam and Eve failed to achieve by eating the forbidden fruit, Christ gives us in the context of the resurrection meal in which he calls us His friends. He gives us access to "all"

The Drug of Immortality

knowledge that comes from God by inviting us to ingest His flesh, the drug of immortality, the fruit of the Tree of Life.

The Hebrew word *sode* expresses friendship with God and is thus at times translated as "friendship" as in Psalm 25:14, but most often as "secret counsel."

The secret counsel that the Lord reveals to His friends is nothing less than the totality of all truth and knowledge. Such knowledge enlightens us to make good judgments in the Council of the Lord in our calling to rule the universe wisely with Christ.

About His "friend" Abraham, the Lord asked rhetorically, "Shall I hide from Abraham what I'm about to do?" (James 2:23; Gen. 18:17). Of course not. And so the Lord revealed *all* to Abraham. Likewise, the Lord held nothing back from Moses, speaking to him face to face as a man speaks with his friend (Ex. 33:11). Moses knew this was God's high intention for you, for me, for all people. So Moses wished for the day when all of the Lord's people would know this level of intimacy, friendship, and empowerment (Num. 11:29).

In the resurrection community of the Church, on each resurrection day, during every celebration of the resurrection meal that Christ hosts for humanity, Moses' wish is fulfilled.

So when you partake of the drug of immortality at the next celebration of the Lord's Supper, ingest faithfully and be transformed totally. It's the smart thing to do.

7

Project Elrond

Nineteenth Week after Pentecost, 2015

Last night Sheila and I went out with our dear friends Thor and Dana Iverson and Wesley Tullis on a little adventure. After our last earthly meal at the Colorado Mountain Brewery, we went to Mars. Why not?

A NASA Secret Counsel Meeting

Much to our delight, deep into the film, mission director Venkat-Vincent Kapoor (Chiwetel Ejiofor), NASA PR director Annie Montrose (Kristen Wiig), Jet Propulsion Laboratory (JPL) director Bruce Ng (Benedict Wong), NASA director Teddy Sanders (Jeff Daniels), and flight director Mitch Henderson (Sean Bean) convene a meeting to consider an out of the box plan cooked up by astrodynamicist Rich Purnell (Donald Glover) to bring astronaut Watney home.

Venkat calls this meeting, "Project Elrond." Wonder why? So did Annie. Here's the scene from the book:

Project Elrond

> "What...is 'Project Elrond'?" Annie asked.
> "I had to make something up," Venkat said.
> "So you came up with 'Elrond'?" Annie pressed.
> "Because it's a secret meeting?" Mitch guessed. "The email said I couldn't even tell my assistant."
> "I'll explain everything once Teddy arrives," Venkat said.
> "Why does 'Elrond' mean 'secret meeting'?" Annie asked.
> "Are we going to make a momentous decision?" Bruce Ng asked.
> "Exactly," Venkat said.
> "How did you know that?" Annie asked, getting annoyed.
> "Elrond," Bruce said. "The Council of Elrond. From Lord of the Rings. It's the meeting where they decide to destroy the One Ring."

It's hilarious that it's Mitch who guesses that Project Elrond is a secret meeting because—and here's where it gets doubly cool, calling for a fist-bump with Thor—Mitch is played by Sean Bean who also starred as Boromir in *The Lord of the Rings: The Fellowship of the Ring* (2001 movie). Boromir is the warrior-statesman who represents Gondor at the *secret counsel* meeting Elrond calls to decide the fate of the One Ring and thus of the world. (No pressure.) When the Council agrees to accept Frodo's chivalric offer to take the One Ring to Mount Doom and destroy it, the following dialogue and action unfold:

> **Boromir**: If this is indeed the will of the Council, then Gondor will see it done.
>
> **Sam** [emerging from his hiding place where he had been eavesdropping on the Council's deliberations and running over to stand by Frodo]: Mr. Frodo's not going anywhere without me.
>
> **Elrond**: No. indeed. It is hardly possible to separate you even when he is summoned to a secret council and you are not.

In that I write a blog series called *Secret Counsel*, and I'm a total *Lord of the Rings* nut, and I would love to join the first band of Mars colonists, you can appreciate the restraint I exercised in the theater last night when I did not stand up and yell at the top my lungs, "Yes! This movie totally *rocks!*"

FUSING THOUGHT AND ACTION

Secret counsel knowledge is not just theoretical and conceptual, but the exercise of a concrete, creative power that brings things into being. *Secret counsel* sacramentally achieves new and radical solutions to real-world problems *before* most people on earth see those solutions manifest.

There are two stages to bringing a thing into being. First, there's its creation in thought. Second, there's its implementation in action. What's peculiar about heroes and immortals of myth and legend is their divinely-derived godlike ability to fuse thought and action into a greater whole. For them thought and action are one and the same. In contrast, mortals are low-spirited scribes who passively spectate and record objective facts in the world around them as they manifest. Scribes are reporters, not creators. Heroes and immortals, by the fusion of thought and action, create what scribes report.

Heroes and immortals know the concrete reality of things before scribes report them.

Jesus knew things and taught as one having authority, not as the scribes (Matt. 7:29). Heroes and immortals, following Jesus' lead, operate out of a divinely-derived authority that automatically brings ideas into being. The power of *secret counsel* knowledge is the power to shape the world by the mere offscouring of one's charisma, giving scribes something to write home about.

Thus, heroes and immortals don't fight *for* a victory not yet won "on earth," but *from* a victory already achieved "in heaven." The world is created, sustained, and ruled by those who have victory in their hearts *before* ever setting foot on the field of battle. What gets worked out in the world of space and time is a certain destiny already foreseen and authored by heroes and immortals in gatherings of *secret counsel*.

Creative knowledge that fuses thought and action is *inherent* to God's nature, which is why what He conceives exists. With God there is no gap between the subjective and the objective. While we have no such *inherent* power, yet because God has made us in His image and likeness we can by grace *inherit* from Him the ability to fuse thought and action as one.

In God's economy, participants in *secret counsel* gatherings conceive "in heaven" the reality of things before they publicly manifest "on earth." As Jesus says, we have the authority to bind and loose on earth only *what we first* bind and loose in heaven (Matt. 16:19).

The primary means by which heroes and immortals bind and loose in heaven is by enacting *secret counsel* first in story and drama, like what happens in novels and movies. For mortals, fantasy isn't real but pretend. But fantasy in the hands of faithful immortals is the power of sanctified imagination to fuse thought and action and build worlds in the language of poetry, epic story, ceremony, liturgy, and ritual.

Embodying God

Over the years, I've come to experience the Liturgy of the Church as *the* high-drama in which our low-spirited mortality is swallowed up by high-spirited immortality, transforming us into storytellers who cannot help but colonize worlds in thought, word, and deed.

THE POWER TO GIVE VISION BEING

The power to give vision being is divine. By Grace we may become partakers of the divine nature and exercise such power as a gift, which some call a *charism*. Because we are created in God's image with this potential, there is therefore a kind of restlessness in us to see the things we can conceive brought into being.

In the Ainulindalë, J.R.R. Tolkien's account of creation in *The Silmarillion*, there is this wonderful passage:

> Then there was unrest among the Ainur [powerful beings created by God who in turn sung creation into being via a Great Music]; but Ilúvatar [God] called to them, and said: 'I know the desire of your minds that what ye have seen should verily be, not only in your thought, but even as ye yourselves are, and yet other. Therefore I say: Eä! Let these things Be!'

Those who live in the zone of *secret counsel* can be shocked that in the chronological unfolding of the world in space and time that what they've conceived has not yet been manifested. To high-spirited creatures for whom thought and action are one, this can take some getting used to. Many entrepreneurs in the business world, for example, operate this way—speaking in the past tense about things they have envisioned before they have come into being in the realm in which mortals live.

Project Elrond

And so the Ainulindalë continues,

> But when the Valar [those of the Ainur who chose to leave "heaven" and continue their work "on earth"] entered into Eä [the universe of space and time] they were at first astounded and at a loss, for it was as if naught was yet made which they had seen in vision, and all was but on point to begin and yet unshaped, and it was dark. For the Great Music had been but the growth and flowering of thought in the Timeless Halls, and the Vision only a foreshowing; but now they had entered in at the beginning of Time, and the Valar perceived that the World had been but foreshadowed and foresung, and they must achieve it.

I've come to see *colonization* as the act of achieving the world that we conceive in places of *secret counsel*.

CULTIVATING TO COLONIZE

The Martian just keeps on giving.

There's a scene in *The Martian* (2015 movie) that ties together themes we're exploring here in this chapter with a blog series I'm writing for CenterPoint, a business Initiative of the Basileia Abbey of St. John. Watney, a botanist by training, figures out a way to take a few potatoes and turn them into a crop so he doesn't starve to death. Documenting his accomplishment on video (in part, for posterity, should he not survive), he combines a little colonization theory with his characteristic humor and wit: "They say once you grow crops somewhere, you have officially 'colonized' it. So technically, I colonized Mars. In your face, Neil Armstrong!"

As I implied in my recent CenterPoint blog, "Listen to the Grass Grow" (www.centerpoint.partners), the rational for "why I farm" is to join with other heroes and immortals in the Kingdom colonization of earth. We have a world to terraform ("farm"), making it just like heaven (Matt. 6:10).

The word *cultivate* is based on the Latin *cultus*, which means "worship." The Divine Liturgy is worship in the form of *cultus*, which in turn gives rise to another form of worship— *culture*. According to the *Oxford English Dictionary*, culture also means "worship," but of a different kind than *cultus*. Crop cultivation is quite literally a form of worship that gives expression to the essence of what starts out as *cultus*. All culture, beginning with agriculture, is *cultus* externalized. *Cultus* sacramentally fuses thought and action as *secret counsel* in the drama of the Liturgy "in heaven" which in turn gives rise to culture "on earth" in colonizing efforts that achieve the world.

Culture is the outworking in space and time of a drama conceived and first enacted ceremonially by heroes and immortals in gatherings for *secret counsel*. While the Liturgy is a fantasy for mortals, the Liturgy is the stage upon which immortals structure and restore the world by eating Christ's flesh and drinking of His blood. Such liturgical acts enact the story of the power of Christ's death and resurrection for the life of the world. Sacramental, liturgical acts of achieving the world are stage one. Colonization is the stage two unfolding of stage one. Heroes and immortals at times can hardly distinguish between these stages.

To make the Garden in Eden a colony of heaven on earth—a beachhead for expanding into all the earth (and to Mars too!)—God commanded Mankind to *cultivate* and keep it (Gen. 2:15). Likewise, as astronaut Watney rightly understood, to cultivate a potato crop is the definitive colonization of a world. "I colonized Mars," he triumphantly says. Once that happens, it only makes sense to enact Project Elrond to bring him home and inspire others to follow in his steps.

Check out *The Martian* for yourself. You'll see what I mean.

8

A GREAT MUSIC

Seventeenth Week after Pentecost, 2015

THERE ARE ASPECTS OF TRUTH that can only be perceived, received, and celebrated in epic stories of myth and legend.

The more I immerse myself in the universal language of myth and legend the more alive Scripture becomes, the more mystically transformative the sacraments and the Liturgy become, and the more clear the speaking of the Holy Spirit becomes.

For years—and I mean for about twenty-four years—I've fallen frustratingly short in my attempts to communicate the *feel* I have for the biblical idea of *secret counsel*. Yes, it's true that "secret counsel" is an English rendering of the Hebrew word *sode*, the idea of which is expressed in the New Testament by the Greek word *mysterion*, which shows up in the mouth of Jesus in the phrase, "the mystery of the kingdom." The equivalent of *sode* and *mysterion* in Latin is *sacramentum* from which we get our word "sacrament." There. Are you inspired now?

But I'm now discovering in myth and legend a power of language, thought, and perception that liberates the wonder of *secret counsel*, the *mystery* of the kingdom, and the *sacraments* of the Church to operate as portals of transfiguration.

THE MUSIC OF THE AINUR

The Ainur are beings of awesome glory and power, created by Ilúvatar (God) in J.R.R. Tolkien's *The Silmarillion*, the collection of epic myths and legends at the foundation of *The Hobbit* and *The Lord of the Rings*. The Ainur are essentially what Scripture calls "thrones or dominions or rulers or authorities" (Col. 1:16).

In *The Silmarillion's* account of creation, Ilúvatar says to the Ainur,

> Of the theme that I have declared to you, I will now that ye make in harmony together a Great Music. And since I have kindled you with the Flame Imperishable, ye shall show forth your powers in adorning this theme, each with his own thoughts and devices, if he will. But I will sit and hearken, and be glad that through you great beauty has been awakened into song.

The essence of *secret counsel* and the *mystery* of the Kingdom is that God's will ("the theme") is not as fixed and restrictive of a thing as the Enemy would deceive us into believing. God wills that in making a Great Music together we participate in shaping the divine theme that shapes your destiny and mine, no less the destiny of all things.

In the place of secret counsel, God kindles us with the Flame Imperishable (the Holy Spirit) to have a say in what His will shall be. The mystery of the Kingdom is that God has given each of us a unique voice, perspective, gifts, and abilities ("powers") to shape the very will of God, "adorning this theme" before it's worked out in the world.

"God Does Nothing Without..."

"For the Lord God does nothing without revealing his secret counsel [sode] to his servants the prophets" (Amos 3:7).

An uninspiring, boring, and theologically erroneous way of understanding Amos 3:7 is that God announces His will to prophets who in turn announce His will to the rest of us. This unimaginative view kills the joy and wonder of perceiving, receiving and celebrating what God truly reveals through sacraments, Scripture and the Spirit—His secret counsel.

God's secret counsel is like music theory, which He wants us to use to shape a Great Music. To shift metaphors, God stocks the pantry and then gives us the go ahead to create recipes to serve up something divine to the world.

Sacraments, Scripture, and the Spirit reveal the will of God in the form of the secret counsel of God, not in the form of formulas. Formulas are for babies. Secret counsel is for "thrones or dominions or rulers or authorities," which is what we are. We are those who at the Lord's Supper eat bread and drink wine "in harmony together...adorning the theme." In the sacrament of communion, Jesus says, "I assign to you, as my Father assigned to me, a kingdom, that you may eat and drink at my table in my kingdom and sit on thrones ruling..." (Luke 22:29-30).

God's rulers don't rule according to formulas but sing a Great Music in accord with the theme God declares through sacraments, in Scripture, and by the Spirit. What's the will of God? The will of God is that we "make in harmony together a Great Music."

God did not instruct Moses to build the Tabernacle according to a formula, but "according to *the pattern*" (i.e., the "theme") shown him on the Mountain (Ex. 25:40). Then the Lord filled others in Israel "with the Spirit of God," giving them the "ability and intelligence, with knowledge and all craftsmanship, to devise artistic designs" to adorn the Tabernacle (Ex. 31:3-4). The Tabernacle was not a rigid institutional structure, but a Great Music.

Likewise, king Ahasuerus did not rule by formula, but called together his friends to draft laws "according to the law" (i.e., the "theme") of the kingdom (Esther 1:15). Constitutional *law* is a theme while legislated *laws* are a Great Music created according to the theme.

Thus, Ilúvatar was glad as the Ainur sang. "And the music and the echo of the music went out into the Void, and it was not void."

THE WILL OF EVIL

But what happens if some knucklehead (including the one who stares back at us in the mirror) decides not to sing in accord with the theme of God's secret counsel? Such a happening is a thing called *evil*. Yes, evil is a power that ruins worlds, lives, and hopes, *but not permanently*. As Gandalf said to Frodo in the Mines of Moria, "There are other forces at work in this world, Frodo, besides the will of evil."

I believe that a good dose of epic myth and legend is just what the doctor ordered to cure us of our fallen tendency to feel that the will of evil can overrule our destiny. Evil is not that powerful.

The will of evil makes its debut in *The Silmarillion* as follows:

> But as the theme progressed, it came into the heart of Melkor to interweave matters of his own imagining that were not in accord with the theme of Ilúvatar; for he sought therein to increase the power and glory of the part assigned to himself.

Melkor, one of the Ainur, goes off the rails, just like Satan did before his visit to Adam and Eve in Genesis 3. The first words out of Satan's mouth introduce disharmony into the music "not in accord with the theme" of God's secret counsel.

But because evil is good twisted, what evil intends, God repurposes for good. As Ilúvatar puts it,

> And thou, Melkor, shalt see that no theme may be played that hath not its uttermost source in me, nor can any alter the music in my despite. For he that attempteth this shall prove but mine instrument in the devising of things more wonderful, which he himself hath not imagined.

It's the nature of Great Music to overcome evil with good. Great Music repurposes what evil twists into things more wonderful than we can imagine.

Conclusion

A famous evangelistic tract came out some years ago declaring, "God has a wonderful plan for your life." What's mind blowing is that God's plan is for you to participate in writing this plan for yourself, others, and the world in accord with "the theme that I have declared to you." Feeling a bit ill-equipped to script something like this?

Don't worry, you can't permanently mess up your destiny or that of anyone else, no less the world's. While temporary messes happen, through these messes "things more wonderful" than we have dared to imagine emerge as new elements of myth and legend in a Great Music.

9

CHANGE YOUR WORLD

Tenth Week after Pentecost, 2015

THERE'S A WONDERFUL SECRET COUNSEL dialog from *The Equalizer* (2014 film) between Robert McCall (Denzel Washington), a retired black ops agent, and his Millennial friend, Alina (Chloë Grace Moretz).

Alina is caught up in the dark world of crime and prostitution but dreams of being a singer.

> **Alina** (*handing McCall a homemade CD of her singing*): Okay, it's not professional. Just tell me what you think. Okay?
> **McCall**: O wow. Alina, the singer.
> **Alina**: You and I know what I really am.
> **McCall**: I think you can be anything you want to be.
> **Alina**: Maybe in your world, Robert. That doesn't really happen that way in mine.
> **McCall**: Change your world!

Alina knows she can't make a change for the better in her ruined, broken world. McCall knows it too and doesn't even suggest she try. Instead, McCall, true to his name, *calls* Alina to do something truly radical—change worlds.

HOPE AND EXCHANGE

Jesus doesn't call us to hope and believe that the "world" can be changed for the better, but to *exchange* one world (kingdom) for another. "The time is fulfilled, and the kingdom of God is at hand; repent and believe in the gospel" (Mk. 1:15). In other words, "Change your world."

Protestants don't need to change into Catholics, nor do Catholics need to change into Protestants. Both Catholics and Protestants need to change worlds; then we can iron out the small stuff.

Democrats don't need to change into Republicans, nor do Republicans need to change into Democrats. Both Democrats and Republicans need to change worlds to embrace true "hope and change," not the nonsense that we should hope to change the Fallen World System for the better.

I could go on. And I will.

Males don't need to change into females, nor do females need to change into males. Changing gender isn't radical enough. Both males and females need to change their world to discover their genuine, authentic selves.

You get the idea. It works for a lot of stuff.

A BIG BLACK BUCKET OF PAINT

One of my favorite Far Side cartoons is the one of the guy strolling the neighborhood with a big black bucket of paint. He paints the words "house" on a house, "tree" on a tree,

Embodying God

"cat" on a cat, and so on. The caption reads, "Now...*That should clear up a few things around here!*"

So, if you would kindly indulge me, there are a few things that need clearing up.

At bottom, there are only two worlds, which are *not* the heavens and the earth.

The heavens are not a "world." Nor is earth a "world." The heavens and the earth are *realms* that *together* form a world. In the beginning, when God made the world, He "created the heavens and the earth" (Gen. 1:1). It takes both realms to make a world.

Furthermore, a world is ruled by "powers in the heavens above" and "kings on the earth below" (Isa. 24:21, NIV). And here's where it gets interesting: There are two entirely different sets of ruling powers and kings. There are good heavenly powers allied with good earthly kings in the world of the Kingdom of God, and there are evil heavenly powers in league with evil earthly kings in the world of the Kingdom of Satan.

Both the Kingdom of God and the Kingdom of Satan, like white and black pieces on a chessboard, are at war over whose world system shall rule creation.

Properly understood, a "world" is an administration, a system of government, a kingdom. The world of the Kingdom of Satan goes by various names, including The First Heavens and the First Earth and Babylon. The world of the Kingdom of God is called The New Heavens and the New Earth, New

Jerusalem, and the Church. Like two opposing teams, these worlds are in conflict. But these worlds are not equals. One is passing away. The other is ascending.

The destruction of the First Heavens and the First Earth is *not* the destruction of the *physical* heavens and earth. The *physical* heavens and earth—the creation—is being transformed just as Jesus' dead body was transformed in the Resurrection. The same body that went into the tomb came out of the tomb, but in a transformed way. The only thing destined for destruction is the *administration* of unrighteous powers in the heavens above in cahoots with wicked kings on the earth below.

Creation's destiny—the future of the physical heavens and earth—is *restoration*, not destruction. The destiny of the First Heavens and the First Earth—the Fallen World System—is *destruction*, not restoration.

There. I hope that clears up a few things.

Conclusion

Mortals set out to change the world only to spend their lives throwing hammers at the moon, for all the good it does.

Immortals change their world and sing the "song of Moses, the servant of God, and the song of the Lamb" (Rev. 15:3).

Listen. Do you hear that?

O wow. It's Alina, the singer.

10

WAYBREAD OF ELVES

Thirteenth Week after Pentecost, 2015

JESUS SAYS, "EVERYONE WHO HAS heard and learned from the Father comes to me" (Jn. 6:45).

But how does God the Father speak?

My spiritual journey these last twelve years has been wonderfully elevated by my encounter with the Convergence Movement, which weaves together in a three-stranded cord God's revelation through sacrament, in Scripture, and by the Spirit.

The Evangelical-Reformed traditions of the Church champion hearing and learning *from God the Son*. As the Word made flesh, the Son speaks prophetically in accord with Scripture, particularly about "things concerning himself" (Lk. 24:27). Nevertheless, this is not how the Father speaks.

The Charismatic and Pentecostal elements of the Church teach us about hearing and learning *from God the Spirit*. The

Spirit speaks to us in anointed and kingly ways, including in dreams, visions, and tongues, "not in plausible words of wisdom, but in demonstration of the Spirit and of power" (1 Cor. 2:4). Nevertheless, this is not how the Father speaks either.

So, how does God the Father speak?

SACRAMENTS AREN'T JUST FOR SUNDAY ANYMORE

The Liturgical-Sacramental dimensions of the Church embrace the Father speaking in priestly, creational, and sacramental ways. "For his invisible attributes, namely, his eternal power and divine nature, have been clearly perceived, ever since the creation of the world, in the things that have been made" (Rom. 1:20). When in worship we use "things that have been made," like bread and wine in communion and water in baptism, we call them sacraments, reminding us that *the whole of creation is sacramental*. Sacraments aren't just for Sunday anymore.

The Father's language is way more wild, controversial, profoundly mystical, and outright outrageous than mortal minds can handle. Thus, to hear and learn from the Father we must first eat what Tolkien tells us is *lembas*, the waybread of Elves.

> "The lembas had a virtue without which they would long ago have lain down to die...[T]his waybread of the Elves had a potency that increased as travellers relied on it alone and did not mingle it with other foods. It fed the will, and it gave strength to endure, and to master sinew and limb beyond the measure of mortal kind." (*Return of the King*)

Embodying God

IT WILL BLOW YOUR MIND

If we can but relax and roll with it, the Father's language invites us to cast mortal caution to the wind and hit the eject button on safe human formulas of truth.

In the wild place of secret counsel, the Father calls us to embrace joyfully the mystical call to chivalric high adventure in the exploration of the limitless possibilities of existence.

Individuals, relationships, companies, and even whole civilizations die due to lack of imagination. Evil's worst nightmare is a human being with a sanctified imagination. All that's necessary for evil to triumph is for good people *not* to use their imagination.

Lest evil have the last word, the Father's voice comes to us in breathtaking ways, starting with our very humanity as made in His image and likeness. If imagination is the ability to think in terms of imagery, then there's no more remarkable image to start with than Mankind—the very image of God Himself.

If you're not yet experiencing shortness of breath over the phrase, "made in His image and likeness," then maybe I can say it another way. God (*Elohim*) has so precisely made us in His image and likeness that Scripture applies the term *elohim*, not just to God, but also to you and me.

When accused of blasphemy for saying, "I am the Son of God" (Jn. 10:36), Jesus defended His unique type of divinity by pointing out that *all people* already share in a God-given, universal kind of human deity. He quoted Psalm 82:6 to make His point, "Is it not written in your Law, 'I said, you are gods'?" (Jn. 10:34). Jesus essentially says, "Don't freak out that I call Myself 'the Son of God,' because the Father, who has 'consecrated and sent' Me into the world, calls *all* human beings gods (*elohim*)."

Could it be that Jesus wasn't *rebuking* His adversaries as much as He was trying to *blow their minds* for their own sake? It's quite refreshing to think that getting our minds blown by God is an essential aspect of "salvation." Sounds fun.

SEE, I HAVE MADE YOU AS A GOD

Some human beings are unrighteous, false gods like Pharaoh, who die like mere mortals (Ps. 82:7). So, in the course of human events, how does the Father deal with human gods gone bad? "And the Lord said to Moses, 'See, I have made you as a god (*elohim*) to Pharaoh, and your brother Aaron shall be your prophet'" (Ex. 7:1).

Not all gods are false gods.

Imagine yourself before baptism like Pharaoh, and then after baptism like Moses. "See, I have made you as a god," says the Lord. That's what the priestly sacrament of baptism is about, no less the sacramental waybread of the Eucharist.

The Father's way of speaking would have us stop being mortals who lick the ungodly humanist boot stomping on our faces. In other words, "don't let yourselves be squeezed into the shape dictated by the present age. Instead, be transformed by the renewing of your minds, so that you can work out what God's will is–what is good, acceptable, and complete" (Rom. 12:2, *The Kingdom New Testament*).

Embodying God

Renewing our minds involves *imagining* the Kingdom of God all over again in light of what the Father is saying. Consider the Lord's Prayer: "Our Father who art in heaven, hallowed be your name. Your kingdom come..." (Matt. 6:9-10). The Kingdom of God is the *Father's* Kingdom. And in regards to the Church, notice that Jesus says He's building His Church upon what *the Father* reveals, not what flesh and blood reveal (Matt 16:17).

If we don't *first* hear and learn what God the Father says, then what God the Son and God the Spirit reveal about the Kingdom tends to get sanitized and sentimentalized by human formulas. Furthermore, failing first to hear from the Father subjects the Church to the unimaginative flesh and blood traditions of men. Such formulas echo the spirit of the age more than heaven. Such formulas try to tame the truth, attempting to make it more palatable to human mortals.

The truth will never be tamed because its nature is to make us wild.

The Apotheosis of George Washington

The special sacraments of the Church teach us *also* to hear and learn from the Father through the general sacraments of immortal epic and mythic story, poetry, art, architecture, and music.

Take architecture, for example. Every capital building in every country of the world is a *temple*. Walk into the rotunda of the United States Capitol Building in Washington, D.C., look up and what do you see? A fresco called, "The Apotheosis of Washington." The mural depicts George Washington ascending into the sky to take his place among the heavenly beings *as a god* (apotheosis). Is this blasphemy? That's debatable.

While "The Apotheosis of Washington" may not be comfortably Evangelical or Charismatic, it has a lot in common with the way the Father speaks about the nature of Mankind. Perhaps there's something here to hear and learn from the Father after all.

May "The Apotheosis of Washington" stir us to jealousy.

DEVELOPING A MYTHOLOGICAL CONSCIOUSNESS

To hear and learn from the Father requires that we develop a mythological consciousness, that is, a mystical imagination. Awakening such vision is the great purpose for which J.R.R. Tolkien strived in *The Hobbit, The Lord of the Rings* and *The Silmarillion*. Tolkien was painfully aware that his beloved British Empire had for some time been dying a slow death due to a lack of imagination. So he served up the waybread of Elves to travelers weary on the journey, even as the Angel of the Lord served the fatigued Elijah. "Arise and eat, for the journey is too great for you" (1 Kings 19:7).

We all need some food for thought now and then.

Epic, mythic story is not pagan *per se*, even though there are pagan myths that would subvert to nefarious ends the great adventure of Mankind becoming like God *in God's way*.

Embodying God

Satan was correct in saying to Eve, "you will be like God" (Gen. 3:5), for the Lord God made Mankind in His image and likeness. Satan's lie—the lie at the root of mythology that fuels pagan idolatry—was that Adam and Eve could become like God *on their own terms* and *not die*. Rule number one in becoming like God is to eat *only* the waybread set before us by our good Father in heaven. "And the Lord God commanded the man, saying, 'You may surely eat of every tree of the garden, but of the tree of the knowledge of good and evil you shall not eat, for in the day that you eat of it you shall surely die'" (Gen. 2:16-17).

While all idolatry is polytheism, not all polytheism is idolatry. There's a fundamental distinction between the novel deity of God (*Elohim*) and the gift of deification—or *theosis*, as the Eastern Church calls it—given by Grace to Mankind. There is a God and you are not Him. Guarding this distinction between the Creator and the creation enables us more comfortably to embrace a sanctified mysticism and mythology of our own.

Mythic story is essential in celebrating the Church as the union in Christ of a type of deified humanity distinct from the unique type of deity that God alone possesses. As long as we maintain this fundamental distinction, then we can explore with joyful abandon what it means to be created by God to be *elohim* like God. You see, I'm a Fundamentalist after all.

Pantheons of gods are an inescapable concept. A culture that forgets and falls out of communion with their "founding fathers" (i.e., priest-god-kings, like George Washington) cease to be a culture. Thus, one of the most important feasts of the

Waybread of Elves

Christian Year is All Saints Day, celebrated on November 1. On All Saints, we connect with that great pantheon of heroes who embody the Kingdom of God—a pantheon we are destined to join. Until we get comfortable with celebrating ourselves, along with the entire Communion of Saints, as priest-god-kings, then we will remain in a spiritual dark age while pagan empires advance against a castrated Christendom.

LEMBAS, THE LEGENDARY WAYBREAD OF ELVES

In the common tongue, the special sacramental gathering of the Church to feast on lembas, the legendary waybread of Elves, is known as the Lord's Supper or the Eucharist. It's fascinating to me that the Eucharistic prayer of the Church is addressed directly to the Father. These special Sunday gatherings train us in the basics of *also* feasting on lembas Monday through Saturday as we hear and learn from the Father through the sacramental structure of creation in general and of our humanity in particular.

Our journey—our Eucharistic *lifestyle*—of growing in likeness to God, "beyond the measure of mortal kind," is too great for us. Therefore, the Lord invites us to His Table, to a secret counsel feast, and bids us to rise from our mortality and eat. "If anyone eats of this bread," says Jesus, "he will live forever" (Jn. 6:51).

As the Elves counseled the members of the *Fellowship of the Ring* in "Farewell to Lórien,"

> Eat little at a time, and only at need. For these things are given to serve you when all else fails. The cakes will keep sweet for many many days, if they are unbroken and left in their leaf-

wrappings, as we have brought them. One will keep a traveler on his feet for a day of long labour, even if he be one of the tall men of Minas Tirith.

May we feast on lembas together and fuel our imaginations for the journey ahead.

Let's go wild.

11

Circle Me, Lord

Maundy Thursday of Holy Week, 2015

"Visualize World Peace" was a popular bumper sticker some years ago. Then some comedian did what we love comedians to do and came up with a good one: "Visualize Whirled Peas."

Here's another: "Visualize World Judgment."

How do you visualize world judgment? What images come to your mind? Noah's Flood? Locusts? Mushroom clouds? Signs in the heavens? The Second Coming?

Encircling Prayer

The ancient Celts visualized world judgment through an interesting form of prayer called a *caim* or encircling prayer. You stand with your arm outstretched, then point with your index finger and draw a circle as you turn in place, praying things like,

> Circle me, Lord. Keep protection near and danger afar.
> Circle me, Lord. Keep light near and darkness afar.
> Circle me, Lord. Keep peace within; keep evil out.

The idea is to draw a circle around yourself and then ask the Lord to put outside the circle all that is evil while keeping all that is good within. The circle represents the world. The *twofold* action of putting "evil out" *and* keeping "peace within" is world judgment, *secret counsel* style. Visualize that.

KEEPING THE WORLD

Jesus did. He visualized world judgment this way:

> "Now is the judgment of this world; now will the ruler of this world be cast out. And I, when I am lifted up from the earth, will draw all people to myself." He said this to show by what kind of death he was going to die (John 12:31-33).

Note the twofold action here. Jesus, as the Second Adam, redraws the world. He casts out the devil beyond the circle while at the same time drawing all people to be near Him within the circle.

The First Adam and his wife, Eve, did not visualize world judgment when the serpent came into the Garden. The Lord commanded Adam to "keep" the Garden (Gen. 2:15). "Keep" in Hebrew is *shamar*, sometimes also translated as "guard," "watch," or "observe." Adam and Eve had the authority to keep the world by praying, "Circle us, Lord. Keep this world according to Your word as we do Your will within and keep the Evil One out."

The First Adam didn't pray this way nor invite his wife to join him in such a prayer. However, the Second Adam does pray this way and invites His bride, the Church, to join Him in praying this way too. He says, "do this" (Lk. 22:19).

THANKSGIVING

I'm writing this on the morning of Maundy Thursday. This day is *the* day of days in the Church Year when we celebrate and remember Jesus giving His bride, the Church, the invitation to join Him *at a meal* in visualizing world judgment.

We often call this meal the Lord's Supper or the Eucharist ("thanksgiving") but do we really fathom what this meal is about?

When we participate in the Lord's Supper, this is what Jesus says it's about:

> You are those who have stayed with me in my trials, and I assign to you, as my Father assigned to me, a kingdom, that you may eat and drink at my table in my kingdom and sit on thrones judging... (Lk 22:29-31).

The Lord's Supper is where the secret counsel for "judging" the world is discussed, hammered out and enacted. "Judging" here doesn't have to do with mushroom clouds, but with making *good decisions*, i.e., judgments.

Visualize world judgment now. What do you see? I see a table, bread and wine, the Lord with us and us with Him having a *conversation* about ruling the universe.

> Circle Colorado Springs, Lord. Keep protection near and danger afar.

Embodying God

> Circle the persecuted Church in Syria and Iraq, Lord. Keep light near and darkness afar.
>
> Circle those who persecute the Church in Syria and Iraq, Lord. Cast out the prince of the world and draw these persecutors to yourself.

As a priest of the Church, when I officiate at the Eucharist, I do what priests the world over do and have done for millennia, ever since Jesus instituted this meal. I lift up the bread and say, "Behold, the Lamb of God who takes away the sin of the world." The people respond, "Lord, have mercy." Then, while continuing to hold up the bread, I tear it in two from top to bottom. Rending the bread in this manner signifies the kind of death Jesus died—the death by which He cast out the prince of the world and now draws all to Himself. That's visualizing world judgment.

Every time I lift up the bread, I recall Jesus' words from John 12, "when I am lifted up."

THE COMPASSING OF GOD

At the end of our services we stand to visualize world judgment. We redraw the circle of the world with our index fingers as a Deacon pronounces this blessing in the form of an encircling ("compassing") prayer:

> The compassing of God be upon you,
>   the compassing of God, of the God of life.
> The compassing of Christ be upon you,
>   the compassing of the Christ of love.
> The compassing of the Spirit be upon you,
>   the compassing of the Spirit of grace.
> The compassing of the Sacred Three be upon you,

Circle Me, Lord

    the compassing of the Sacred Three protect you,
    the compassing of the Sacred Three preserve you.

Now that's visualizing world judgment.

May the Lord encircle you this day.

12

JANE AUSTEN RULES!

Sixth Week After Pentecost, 2015

WHEN LEFT TO MY OWN DEVICES I tend to indulge in Star Trekish type stories. But alas, I'm married to a Jane Austen enthusiast.

What at first appears to the casual observer as a divergent taste in storytelling arts and entertainment between Sheila and me is, in fact, more fundamentally the same than different.

What does the romantic fiction of Jane Austen have in common with the science fiction of Gene Roddenberry? Plenty. Both romantic fiction and science fiction shine a spotlight upon *the key* to experiencing the divine sacramentally, exploring Scripture meaningfully, and moving in the power of the Spirit transformationally.

Romantic fiction and science fiction give us *the key* that puts into proper perspective rulings like those of late by the U.S. Supreme Court redefining marriage.

Jane Austen Rules!

The key? Heroism.

A TALE OF TWO SPIRITUALTIES

There are two spirits at war for your soul and mine: the heroic spirit and the elegiac (i.e., an unsanctified, pessimistic and sorrowful) spirit. Each gives rise to a different city. Heroism gives rise to New Jerusalem. Elegiacism gives rise to Babylon.

While there is a place for *sanctified* mourning and sorrow— there is, after all, an entire book in the Bible called Lamentations—the elegiac spirit I'm taking about here is one that engages in *unsanctified* mourning and sorrow over *evil* things lost. It thus sees no point in forming a "Fellowship of the Ring" to destroy evil. Like Saruman, the elegiac spirit surrenders to evil and joins with it, thinking evil is a normal and permanent fixture in the universe.

In contrast, heroic consciousness forms alternative worlds through covenantal alliances, charting in secret counsel with others the noble, chivalric path of destroying evil and restoring all things ruined by evil.

Mr. Darcy's covenantal union with Elizabeth and Spock's teamwork and friendship with Kirk and McCoy are heroic alternatives to all things elegiac. Such heroes bravely succeed in creating a more noble world.

The elegiac spirit aims no higher than to manage the broken world of Babylon, settling for institutions that capitalize on treating sickness instead of championing wellness and economic systems that distribute wealth instead of creating it.

Embodying God

The elegiac spirit is the sad soul of Babylon's villains. At the Fall of Babylon the wicked kings and merchants of the earth elegiacally "weep and mourn for her" (Rev. 18:9-20). That right there is the best definition of this interesting but unusual word, "elegiac"—weeping and mourning over Babylon's fall. Babylonian villains aren't sorry for the evil they have done, but because the evil they attempted has failed.

Heroism is born when elegiac prodigals come to their senses in the pig pen and determine to return to their father's house. In the Father's House we do not mourn and weep like Babylon's villains do when the enemies of sin, Satan and death are destroyed, but we rejoice as heroes.

Then there are Babylon's victims who mistakenly think that supreme courts rule the land, not Jane Austen.

Elegiac victims, like the children of Israel after their deliverance from Egypt, pine for leeks and onions by the Nile. This brand of elegiacism fondly remembers the days when Pharaoh pitched his slaves a little straw to help them make the bricks that built his empire. Wasn't that nice of Pharaoh? The fear of leaving that broken world and crossing the wilderness to enter the Promised Land resulted in that entire generation dying in the desert. "Now these things took place as examples for us, that we might not desire evil as they did" (1 Cor. 10:6).

Of all who left Egypt, only heroic Joshua and Caleb crossed Jordan into the Promised Land.

Jane Austen Rules!

A MANIFESTO OF HEROIC ENTHUSIASM

My central purpose in everything I write is to crush the elegiac spirit with one blow after another of heroic spirituality. With every *Secret Counsel* blog I write I upload a piece of heroic music for my readers' listening enjoyment. I figure it will connect us somehow because I write my blogs immersed in this music.

What's more, I crave the smell of the incense we burn during our Abbey worship services in my nostrils. I adore the grain of the Eucharistic bread and the silk of the Eucharistic wine on my tongue. These things enthuse me.

The elegiac spirit knows nothing of enthusiasm.

I love the word "enthusiasm." It's a composite of *en* ("in") and *theos* ("God"). To be enthused is to be ingodded. Enthusiasm is the normal, natural state of creatures like us—creatures made in the image and likeness of God. An elegiac consciousness is foreign and unnatural to all that it means to be authentically human. As I've come to see it, discipleship is cultivating our awesome God-given capacity for heroic enthusiasm.

Just ask Joshua and Caleb. They will tell you that Jane Austen and Spock are of those who declare,

> We believe collapsing civilizations are the problem for which colonies of heaven are the solution.
>
> In the darkness we say, "Let there be light."

Embodying God

We dare to imagine all things in our good yet broken world restored.

We assemble.

We cultivate wisdom in the secret places of the world where heroes gather, not to be noticed, but to map dangerous paths of obedience into the heart of darkness, knowing the cost.

We fear no evil, not even in the Valley of the Shadow of Death because in death we exhaust evil, putting death to death.

Resurrection power is not a concept to us, but a reality we have tasted. It tastes like chivalric love triumphant.

(Epic Living, p. 68)

Don't be fooled. A Supreme Court captured by the elegiac spirit of the age doesn't rule. Jane Austen rules! And as I'm quick to remind Sheila, so does Spock.

Live long and prosper.

13

Colony of Heaven

Eighth Week after Pentecost, 2015

The Church on earth is a colony of heaven's citizens commissioned to heavenize earth.

I started believing this twenty-five years ago. Ever since I've been on a journey to live as a free citizen of the Kingdom of God on earth now. I refuse to be a subject of the Fallen World System where my highest ambition is merely to go to heaven when I die.

Charting a fresh path today for how to be a colony of heaven on earth begins by engaging in a little *secret counsel* with our friends. One of those friends is Johannes Wolff, Jr., currently a member of the Church in heaven.

From Subject to Citizen

On July 25, 1889, Sheila's great-grandfather, Johannes Wolff, Jr. appeared before the Clerk of the District Court of McIntosh County, Dakota Territory, before whom he

...made oath that he was born in Russia on or about the year eighteen hundred and sixty eight, that he immigrated to the United States and landed at the port of New York on or about the month of April in eighteen hundred and eighty five; that it is bona fide his intention to become a CITIZEN OF THE UNITED STATES, and to renounce forever all allegiance and fidelity to any foreign Prince, Potentate, State or Sovereignty whatever, and particularly to the Czar of Russia whereof he is a subject, and that he will support the Constitution and Government of the United States.

Johannes was born a German colonist in Russia. Beginning in the late 1700's, waves of German colonists immigrated to Russia at the invitation of Catherine the Great, who was of German descent and who became the renowned, longest-reigning female ruler of Russia. But on June 4, 1871, when Johannes was about three, Czar Alexander II revoked the rights that Catherine had granted the colonists, turning Johannes and his family into *subjects* of the Russian Empire.

Refusing to be subjects in someone else's empire, Johannes and his family took a page out of colonist Noah's book, got on a ship and left behind the old world for the New World.

BAPTISM REVISITED

The document Johannes Wolff signed on July 25, 1889 is the civil equivalent of a baptismal certificate rightly understood.

Baptism is not a rite by which individuals publically declare that they are "saved" and going to heaven when they die. Through the waters of baptism the Church collectively declares that the person being baptized is now accountable to renounce forever all allegiance and fidelity to the powers of the Fallen World System, and particularly to the Prince of the Fallen World System, Satan, whereof we have been subjects, and that the one baptized is now a citizen of the Kingdom of God on earth who serves Emperor Jesus, His Constitution, and His Government.

Noah and his family passed through the baptismal flood waters to colonize the New World. Israel did not go through the baptismal waters of the Red Sea for any reason less than to be constituted as a colony of heaven on earth at Mount Sinai. The Lord then commissioned Israel to take heaven's culture revealed on Mount Sinai with them through the baptismal waters of the Jordan River and heavenize the Promised Land.

Colonists bring the culture of their homeland with them to transform whatever land they land in accordingly. While exiles conform to the culture of their captors, colonists invite their would-be captors to convert to their culture or let them go. The Lord was a perfect Gentlemen in telling Pharaoh through Moses, "Let my people go." After Pharaoh refused, ten plagues later Israel left anyway.

Captors beware. Colonists be brave. God favors colonists.

"WE ARE A COLONY OF HEAVEN"

The ancient city of Philippi took its name from Philip of Macedon, Alexander the Great's father. Caesar Augustus refounded Philippi—a city in the midst of "barbarian" territory—as a colony of Rome for Roman military vets in honor of their service. Philippi thus became a beachhead of Roman life and values that served as a model and training ground for people seeking Roman citizenship.

Philippi's status as a colony of Rome is the background to Paul's statement to the Church at Philippi, "We are a colony [*politeuma*] of heaven…" (Phil. 3:20a, Moffatt translation). Other English translations render this phrase as, "Our citizenship is in heaven." The idea is that the Church on earth is a commonwealth or colony of heaven's citizens.

The Greek word *politeuma* is where we get the English words political and politics.

Heaven's politics or *politeuma* make the Church a *polis* (a "city") called to embody on earth heaven's worship, culture, music, customs, lifestyle, family values, story, language, art, science, clothes, government, law, mercy, justice, constitution, calendar, economics, and education.

Thank you, Johannes "Noah" Wolff, Jr. for helping us to see that heavenly citizenship isn't just for heaven anymore.

14

WHAT'S YOUR VALUE?

Second Sunday in Lent, 2015

MY FRIEND AND FELLOW BASILEIAN in Wales, Presbyter Tim Abel, promotes a secret counsel alternative to the popular practice of counseling.

As a Soul Friend, Tim is forming a colony of heaven on earth by giving people a place to belong to believe instead of requiring them to believe before they can belong.

Tim doesn't do multiple counseling sessions with people. He typically meets with someone just once, rarely twice. It doesn't matter if they are Christian believers or nonbelievers. Tim gets things headed in a transformative direction by asking one simple question: "On a scale from one to ten, with ten being the highest, what's your value?

Think about it. How would you answer that question for yourself?

Embodying God

THE DAY OF YOUR BIRTH

Tim says, "Most people say, 'I'm a six or a seven.'" Very rarely does anyone say, "I'm a ten" or "I'm a one." But it's the second, follow-up question that Tim asks where things get interesting: "What was your value on the day of your birth?"

At this point, people cock their heads sideways, ponder a moment, and then in a flash of insight say, "On that day I was a ten!"

"But on the day of your birth," Tim says, "you hadn't done anything, good or bad. Nor had anyone done anything good or bad to you. However, on the day of your birth you were a ten? How can this be?"

Like the sun coming up after a long, cold night, Tim says that people begin to transform physically in front of him. It dawns on them that their value isn't determined by what they have done to others (good or bad) or what other individuals or even systems have done to them (good or bad).

HOW A TEN WALKS

At this point, Tim will have the person stand up and walk across the room. "Show me," he says, "how a person walks who is a ten." Tim then returns to the original question: "So, on a scale of one to ten, what's your value *today*?" The answer comes forth, "I'm a ten!"

To declare, "I'm a ten!" is radical stuff because such a confession is a vital step in changing worlds—of leaving the

Fallen World System behind in exchange for the Kingdom of God. Heroes change worlds; they don't merely try to get along in Babylon. Thus, heroes transform the creation in outward, visible ways, which is a reflection of choosing to change their inner world in unseen ways.

Then, to be sure the person has thoroughly got it, Tim asks, "So what's Hitler's value as a person on a scale of one to ten?" When the person says, smiling and shaking their head at the same time, "He would be a ten too," then Tim knows the person he's working with has had a breakthrough. Now the person is ready, willing and able to start taking responsibility for his or her life like never before and move forward into their destiny and become a colonist of new worlds.

THE CELTIC WAY

What Tim does is "The Celtic Way of Discipleship." The ancient Celtic Christian communities were colonies of heaven, "belong to believe" environments, where unbelievers became disciples and members of the colony *before* they were believers. That's what belong to believe means. Can we handle it?

What Tim models is the kingdomcultural alternative to the two false alternatives of making "converts" and syncretism. (Please note that I put the word "converts" in quotes here to indicate that I'm using it in its popular, twisted and mistaken sense, not in a positive way whatsoever.)

"Converts" are people who believe to belong, but who never get out of Babylon or get Babylon out of them. While the souls of "converts" are saved for heaven, they have little to no feel for what it means to *belong* to a colony right now that is heavenizing earth. "Converts" are *not* colonists of a heavenly city, but subcultural exiles in Babylon, living in holes in the ground in someone else's city.

Let us who are Christians repent daily of being "converts." Lord have mercy!

Then there's syncretism. About 99% of the time, those who promote "believe to belong" forms of evangelism and the Church, mistake the "belong to believe" approach of making disciples for syncretism. Let me give you a practical instead of a technical definition of syncretism. The ancient Roman Empire was syncretistic. You could believe whatever you wanted about gods, goddesses, powers, angels, demons, rocks, cows, the sun, the moon, the stars, and even "God," so long as you affirmed, "Caesar is Lord." As long as you could demonstrate your submission to the declaration, "Caesar is Lord," then you could belong to Roman society and believe whatever the heck you wanted.

And here's the thing about Caesar and syncretistic Rome—they don't care if we make "converts." What they can't tolerate, however, is if we make *disciples* in a "belong to believe" kind of way. Disciples know they are tens and tens don't make good slaves.

An Alternative

Disciples are colonists of an alternative, heavenly empire called the Kingdom of God. The Kingdom of God is not a bunch of principles to believe in, but a society of colonies to belong to. It's all about Word *made flesh*, not just words said.

What's Your Value?

We've come full circle. Today, much of the western world is Rome 2.0. "Converts" who keep their religion to themselves on Sundays are not a problem to modern Roman authorities––authorities who enforce a twenty-first-century form of syncretism through the power of the state.

The Fallen World System in all of its incarnations—call it Rome, Babylon or whatever—is a form of society that has no solution to the problem of evil. Thus, "converts" *flee* from evil while syncretism *embraces* ("celebrates") evil in all its varied forms. "Converts" are so heavenly minded they are no earthly good and syncretism is so earthly minded that it has forgotten about (the third) heaven altogether.

Through repentance, disciples take responsibility for the evil they have done to others. And by forgiving, disciples also choose to be defined and devalued no longer by the evil done unto them. Disciples are those who have entered into the s*ecret counsel* of a new form of humanity in Christ whose mission is to exhaust evil by overcoming it with good.

Thank you, Tim, for opening a door to the Kingdom of God for believers and unbelievers alike in your secret counsel alternative to counseling in Babylon. What you're doing gives me hope, courage, boldness, and humility to imagine, cultivate and launch colonies of heaven on earth for people everywhere who confess, "I'm a ten!"

15

SOMETHING BIG'S HAPPENING

Feast of St. Patrick, 2015

IMAGINE WHAT WOULD HAVE happened if after the serpent asked Eve, "Did God actually say…?" (Gen. 3:1), Eve had said, "Hold your question, Mr. Serpent. Instead of just you and I conversing about that, let's have my husband, Adam, and the Lord God join us. Then, all four of us can enter into this secret counsel meeting and determine what 'God actually' said and what it all means."

Things would have turned out a lot differently if Eve had done that. The Bible would only be three chapters long. Instead, we have an additional 1,186 chapters (plus the last half of Genesis 3) laying out what happened next. It's one mess of a fascinating story.

PASSION

What happened next is that Adam and Eve's passions became disordered. God made us in His image and likeness with a passion for being "like God." The two trees in the midst of the Garden—the Tree of Life and the Tree of the Knowledge of Good and Evil—are two radically different choices or paths for pursuing this passion. If we choose to become like God on God's terms, then our passions are channeled appropriately. If we elect to become like God on our own terms, then our passions become twisted and disordered. We become insatiable, always craving more, but never having enough.

Ever since Adam and Eve's passions got hijacked by the devil, you, me, and the rest of the human race *in Adam* have been trying to become like God on our own terms. But it's hard work being like God, especially when we lack the attributes. Eventually, we fallen mortals get tired of trying. Then something big happens—we come to our senses.

"But when he came to himself, he said, 'How many of my father's hired servants have more than enough bread, but I perish here with hunger!'" (Lk. 15:17).

THE WAVE

We live in a moment of history when an enormous wave of people are coming to their senses all at the same time. Ready to catch the wave?

Each of the last four generations has become progressively more disassociated from modern and post-modern versions of the Church, family and political institutions than the generation before. For example, while 86% of Millennials (18 to 33) say they believe in God, they are less affiliated with the Church than Xers (34 to 49) who are less affiliated than Boomers (50 to 68) who are less affiliated than the so-called

Silent Generation (69 to 86). This progressive decline is what a collapse of civilization looks like. And some civilizations need to collapse.

When Adam and Eve ate from the Tree of the Knowledge of Good and Evil they launched the civilization or Kingdom of Man, the direct competitor to the Kingdom of God. One of these civilizations has a future; the other does not. One is collapsing; the other is rising. Something big's happening.

Reset

The Incarnation hit the reset button on what went off the rails at the serpent's secret counsel session with Adam and Eve in Genesis 3.

The fundamental rule of any secret counsel meeting is that the host asks his or her guests questions, not the other way around. Thus, instead of the Lord inviting us to His Table where we ask questions and He gives us answers, He asks us questions and then listens to our answers. Such conversation is thrilling and terrifying at the same time, which is the inescapable quandary of being an adult.

By asking us questions and listening to our answers, the Lord treats us as adults created in His image and likeness with a passion for being like Him. The serpent craftily counterfeited this approach to divine hospitality by inviting Adam and Eve to a meal of forbidden fruit where he asked the questions and they answered. He played them and enslaved them to their passions.

Something Big's Happening

FASTING AND FEASTING

The Lord's plan to teach Adam and Eve to master their passions was simple. It involved *fasting* from the Tree of the Knowledge of Good and Evil and *feasting* with Him from all the other trees, especially the Tree of Life. "And the Lord God commanded the man, saying, 'You may surely eat of every tree of the garden, but of the tree of the knowledge of good and evil you shall not eat, for in the day that you eat of it you shall surely die'" (Gen. 2:16-17). But Adam and Eve broke the fast and broke the world.

Nevertheless, the Lord didn't stop treating Adam and Eve as adults after they sinned. Immediately, after the infamous, counterfeit secret counsel session with the serpent, the Lord called together a genuine secret counsel. He opened this gathering not with one, but with *four questions*. The Lord didn't lecture Adam and Eve about good and evil, but asked, "Where are you?" "Who told you…?" "Have you eaten…?" and "What is this that you have done?" (Gen. 3:9, 11, 13). With these questions, the Lord opened up *a conversation*.

Conversation *with the Lord and each other* in response to His questions is the Lord's gentle, fatherly, patient way of bringing us to the knowledge of the truth about good and evil. "And the Lord's servant must not be quarrelsome but kind to everyone, able to teach, patiently enduring evil, correcting his opponents with gentleness. God may perhaps grant them repentance leading to a knowledge of the truth, and they may come to their senses and escape from the snare of the devil, after being captured by him to do his will" (2 Tim. 2:24-26).

MYSTERY

The Lord doesn't impose formulaic definitions of truth upon us. We do that to ourselves by following Adam and Eve's example of eating from the Tree of the Knowledge of Good and Evil. But we live at a time in history where each progressive generation is refusing more and more to follow Adam and Eve's example. You can feel a wave of sanity breaking out.

The so-called "wisdom" of the Tree of the Knowledge of Good and Evil turns truth into a formula that kills mystery and conversation. Truth is not a formula. It can't be reduced and restricted to a formula. Ultimately, truth is a Person who calls Himself "the Truth" (Jn. 14:6). And His Body, the Church, is the pillar and ground of the truth (1 Tim. 3:15). Flesh that eats from the Tree of Life embodies the truth. But the traditions of men create formulas for everything—the Church, marriage, politics and even God. Every generation since WWII demonstrates a decreasing tolerance for formulas.

Today, uttering words and phrases like "church," "the institution of marriage," "truth," etc. cause people to break out in allergic reactions. Tree of Knowledge definitions abound. We've tried all kinds of formulas, for example, in regards to the Church—the megachurch, the house church, the local church, the parachurch, the mission church and so on. Millennials are the best at smelling Kingdom of Man formulas from a mile off and want nothing to do with them. Thanks be to God!

Something Big's Happening

Forbidden fruit never satisfies. The more we eat, the hungrier we get. We're at a turning point. Something big's happening. We're losing a taste for formulas. The prodigal son is coming to his senses.

16

Dangerous Paths Taken

Transfiguration Sunday, 2015

SOMETHING DIVINE HAPPENED on our February 9 flight back to Colorado from the 2015 Basileia Convocation in Wales.

I packed in four action-adventure movies: *Fury*, *The Equalizer*, *Guardians of the Galaxy*, and *Hercules*.

Although binging on four movies in a row seated in a chair in the sky at 40,000 feet while flying over one of Earth's oceans at 600 miles per hour between two continents is divinely amazing in its own way, that's not what I'm talking about.

Fury, *Equalizer*, *Guardians*, and *Hercules* each have a remarkable secret counsel scene at a pivotal point in their respective story lines. It corresponds to Transfiguration Sunday, celebrated in this Year of Our Lord 2015 on February 15.

Dangerous Paths Taken

TRANSFIGURATION

Providentially, I'm writing this today on the afternoon of Transfiguration Sunday, 2015. I love it when this happens.

In all great stories, there is a point where the hero and his or her friends make a costly choice. Contrary to the instinct for self-preservation, they take dangerous paths into the heart of darkness to destroy evil and save the world. More precisely, this choice involves separating evil from what it has ruined to *destroy* the evil and *restore* all that evil has ruined. This *twofold* form of victory is ultimately embodied in the *Christus Victor* story.

> We cultivate wisdom in the secret places of the world where heroes gather, not to be noticed, but to map dangerous paths of obedience into the heart of darkness, knowing the cost. We fear no evil, not even in the Valley of the Shadow of Death because in death we exhaust evil, putting death to death. ("Our Manifesto," *Kingdom Superheroes.*)

In *Fury* (2014 movie), for example, the five-man crew of a Sherman tank in WWII, led by battled hardened Don "War Daddy" Collier, get cut off and isolated in enemy territory. After their tank (named *Fury*) is immobilized, the crew considers abandoning it and fleeing for their lives ahead of three hundred German SS soldiers descending on their position. Collier determines to remain with the tank and fight but releases the rest of his crew to flee for their lives into the woods. However, though outnumbered and outgunned, each of the crew, one by one count the cost and also decide to stay and fight. A member of the crew, whose first name is—I'm not kidding—Boyd, quotes from Isaiah 6:8, "Also I heard the voice of the Lord, saying: 'Whom shall I send, and who will go for Us?' Then I said, 'Here am I! Send me.'"

There are also similar "here-am-I-send-me" scenes in *The Equalizer*, *Guardians of the Galaxy*, and *Hercules*.

Since the flight from London to Denver was only about ten hours, I didn't have time to squeeze in yet a fifth movie, *The Fellowship of the Ring*, that has one of my favorite secret counsel scenes of all time—the Council of Elrond. At the Council of Elrond, as I've written elsewhere, "Frodo chooses to carry the Ring to Mount Doom" just as Jesus—in His Transfiguration Sunday council meeting with Moses and Elijah—determined "to carry the cross to Mount Calvary" (*Epic Living*, p. 39).

SECRET COUNSEL

I first ran across this mysterious, sacramental, covenantal concept of secret counsel in 1990. For the last twenty-five years, I've been on a quest to understand better and, through the Church, apply this wondrous idea to all areas of thought and life. One of the milestones in this quest came about just last year after ten years of work alongside my fellow Basileians. During Pascha (Easter) 2014, we published the first edition of *The Constitution of Basileia*, which expresses what the Lord has made known to us in the secret place of the Council of the Lord.

This phrase, "secret counsel" is an English translation of the Hebrew word *sode*, which appears in passages like Jeremiah 23:18, Amos 3:7, and Psalm 25:14. Most English translations of Jeremiah 23:18 render it as "counsel," while many translations of the Amos passage say "secret." English Bibles often translate *sode* in Psalm 25:14 as "friendship," sometimes with a footnote saying, "Or secret counsel."

The Hebrew word *sode* means the same as the New Testament Greek word *mysterion* ("mystery"). It also means the same as the Latin word *sacramentum* ("sacrament"), which brings us full circle as to why translators of *sode* in Psalm 25:14 often render it as "friendship."

Jesus says in John 15:15, while instituting the sacrament of the Lord's Supper, "No longer do I call you servants, for the servant does not know what his master is doing; but I have called you friends, for all that I have heard from my Father I have made known to you."

The Lord makes His secret counsel known to His friends in gatherings that may be pictured both metaphorically and literally as sitting together at a table. This is precisely what Jesus was doing with His disciples in John 15:15.

Keeping John 15:15 in mind, Psalm 25:14 takes on a fresh feel: "The friendship [or secret counsel] of the Lord is for those who fear him, and he makes known to them his covenant." The covenant is the *pattern* of authority by which worlds are made, and when the covenant is broken, unmade.

May we enter into discussions as friends around the Table to explore the mystery of the Kingdom together.

Sometimes, we might even talk about a movie or two…or four.

17

Faith in Humanity

Second Week of Pascha (Easter), 2015

THE GREATER MYSTERY IS GOD'S faith in humanity, not humanity's faith in God.

I would like to offer to guide you into a prayerful encounter with God's faithfulness to your humanity after making a few introductory remarks about this compelling thought.

As I was driving off the other day, one of our neighbors ran up to my car to tell me something. I rolled the window down to hear her say that because of a small thing Sheila and I had done for her that we had restored her "faith in humanity."

I said, "You're welcome," drove off, and have been pondering that ever since.

Having faith in God doesn't magically make the world a better place. Having God's faith in humanity does.

Faith in Humanity

God is a devout humanist as evidenced by His creation of mankind in His image, the Incarnation, the Resurrection of Christ, and the Church.

IN HIS IMAGE

What remains the greater astounding truth is not the sad fact that in Adam we idolatrously create God in our image, but the glorious fact that God has created you and me in His image.

C.S. Lewis called this fact, "The Weight of Glory." On June 8, 1942, in a sermon by that title, Lewis said,

> It is a serious thing to live in a society of possible gods and goddesses, to remember that the dullest and most uninteresting person you talk to may one day be a creature which, if you saw it now, you would be strongly tempted to worship.

THE INCARNATION

Adam and Eve chose to become "like God" on their own terms, resulting in the corruption of God's image in them and all their descendants. But immediately (see Genesis 3:15), God determined to restore His image in mankind through the Incarnation.

As Athanasius, Bishop of Alexandria said nearly 1,700 years ago, God in Christ became "incarnate" that we might be "ingodded."

The Resurrection

While Jesus is the Savior of all in His Incarnation, He is especially the Savior of those who believe in His death and resurrection.

The Resurrection supremely demonstrates God's faith in humanity. This faithfulness of God extends to the depths of Hades. The Paschal Matins of the Orthodox Church proclaims, "To earth hast thou come down, O Master, to save Adam: and not finding him on earth, Thou hast descended into Hades, seeking him there."

The Church

The Lord's faith in humanity builds the Church, not humanity's faith in God.

Scripture paints a picture of secret counsel as a divine-human conversation where God asks the questions of us instead of us of Him. He then listens. God listening to us answer His questions is a most mysterious expression of His faith in humanity. It causes you to wonder.

In a secret counsel gathering with His disciples, as told in Matthew 16, Jesus asked them a question and then listened for their answer. He asked, "But who do you say that I am?" (v. 15). On behalf of himself, the disciples, and all humanity, Peter gave more than just a technically correct answer. Jesus discerned that Peter did not speak what "flesh and blood" had revealed, but according to our "Father who is in heaven" (v. 17). For this reason, Jesus called human, fallible, finite

Peter the "rock" upon which He would build His Church (v. 18).

Peter is every person. It was Peter, after all, in his first epistle, who calls us all living stones (1 Pet. 2:5).

Praying Without Words

Though evil has warped God's image in us, God's commitment to restore your humanity and mine remains. God's commitment takes the form of the Incarnation, the Resurrection, and the Church, each a spiritually physical and bodily reality, like ourselves.

Spirituality that is bodily physical is authentic, genuine and transformational. So, I invite you to pray with me in a form of prayer without words. Praying without words, at least in my experience, has been transformational in teaching me to cultivate a deep awareness of the initiative of God who comes to us as Word made flesh. He comes as light into the darkness, and the darkness cannot overcome this light.

First, get into a quiet place and plan to be there for at least twenty minutes. We're going on a journey through a valley—the Valley of the Shadow of Death. The path of return to the house of the Lord passes through this valley. Therefore, we must go *through* it, not *around* it. The Lord will be with us, and we will fear no evil.

Imagine a dark time, even the darkest time in your life. It could be a season, a moment, or a situation in which you experienced the full weight of evil and death crushing you, immobilizing you, cutting you off from hope and light. Step into that place, this prison of darkness and death, and wait for a moment.

Now see the Lord shining like the sun approaching you. He's looking at you. Look at Him. He comes and stands next to you, puts His arm around you and invites you to lift your eyes and see into the distance. You see the family lines of your mother and your father branching out from you, going back in time. You see generation after generation of the human family from which you've come. The Lord says, "Now watch this!" Pulsing waves of light wash backward through the generations, healing brokenness, casting out demons, forgiving sins, and slamming shut portals of darkness.

The backward movement of the pulsing light slows, then reverses and starts rushing toward you. The light forms a mighty river that passes through you. The Lord takes your hand and turns you around from the past to the future. As this stream of light passes through you, it washes over the people in your life today, including friends and family, even your enemies. As you look to the horizon, you see waves of light washing over generations yet unborn—generations directly connected with you by blood and the covenant.

This past, present and future restoration of the humanity that forms you and that you are in continuity with is the reality of the Incarnation, the Resurrection, and the Church made manifest. The Lord transforms the darkness of generational curses into a light-river of generational blessings. Deposited into your family lineages is the treasure of the ages. This treasure is the inheritance that evil sought to steal, kill and destroy, but which the Lord restores to you. This legacy is alive and flowing to you and through you like a river.

Faith in Humanity

To adapt a saying attributed to St. Francis, "Pray at all times and if necessary use words." I commend this way of prayer to you and encourage you to make it a lifestyle practice.

HIS FAITHFULNESS, NOT OURS

I write this during the Second Week of Pascha (Easter) in which the Gospel reading for Sunday is from John 20 and includes the account of Thomas. Thumbs up to Thomas. I love Thomas. He insisted he wouldn't believe unless he touched Jesus' bodily resurrected physical humanity. Our day sorely needs more of this sort of spirituality. I need more of it.

It's not your faith or my faith in God, but His in us that is at the heart of all authentic secret counsel encounters with the Living God. We are His idea, not our own.

"His faithfulness, not ours, has saved us…" (Gal. 2:16, *The Passion Translation*).

Grace to you.

Afterword

First Sunday of Advent, 2015

Now that I've finished this book, I have a better understanding of why I wrote it.

While I've had nothing but fun this last year stumbling upon one serendipitous example after another of humanity and divinity intersecting, there's a larger purpose I've been pursuing.

This book is a call to all who already see God embodied in and around them to join and form colonies of heaven on earth where yet even more people can belong to believe. Embodying God is not something that we must work for, but the starting point that we work from. Communities formed on this basis liberate the artist and the scientist in each of us to bravely exhaust evil and brilliantly advance the restoration of all things.

For whatever reason, some of us are already predisposed to the mystery of the Kingdom more than not. While that

Afterword

predisposition no doubt isn't as developed as we'd like, at least we're *awake* to the immanence of God *already* embodied in and around us. We're pilgrims, not on a search for something we lack, but on a quest to celebrate, cultivate, and adorn an inheritance we've already received.

We're already mystically connected with the eternal community of angels and archangels and of the spirits of just men made perfect—a community that transcends the boundaries of chronological time and geographic space. Jesus told the Samaritan woman of the coming hour "when neither on this mountain nor in Jerusalem will you worship the Father" (Jn. 4:21). For us, this day of worshiping the Father everywhere was ushered in with the last sunrise. Now what?

Now we find each other, invite still others, and celebrate, cultivate, and adorn the new world *together*.

I suppose this book is my way of shouting out in a crowd, "May I have your attention, please! Who else here feels like you were born out of time? Who feels like you belong to a different world, not the one so many carelessly and casually call the 'real' world? Who here doesn't fit with this so-called 'real' world because you're already living in another? If that's you, if you're one of those artists or scientists (or both) who yearn to unite with others in the great mission of embodying God in colonies of heaven on earth, then would you please raise your hand so I can see you. Thank you. I see that hand! And I see that hand too! Thank you."

These are the kinds of "altar calls" I like to lead.

Embodying God

"Just As I Am" is a hymn dear to my heart in a nostalgic kind of way. My Grandpa Boyd E. Morris and I watched a lot of Billy Graham together on TV on many a summer night at the Morris Ranch during my childhood. Nevertheless, my altar call music of choice includes *Lord of the Rings* pieces like, "The Bridge of Khazad Dum," "The Council of Elrond," and "A Storm is Coming." You get the idea.

If you and I already know each other, then please also know this—I pray for you all the time. And if we don't know each other (yet), then I want you to know something too—I pray for you all the time as well. I hope to meet you soon. And would you please pray for me too?

I'm a big believer in praying for each other as the vital first step in coming to the altar of the Lord's Table together. Minor barriers like space and time may separate us in small ways, but praying for each other actualizes a much deeper connection that's already ours by Grace. We're already providentially connected in the quest to form colonies of heaven on earth. This is our starting point.

Perhaps we won't meet face-to-face until some future age. But I hope to see you sooner than later. Sooner would be good.

Let's go into the hospitality business together and create communities that *first* host the presence of God, then each other, and finally our guests—fellow pilgrims looking for a place to belong to believe.

Let's create communities of sanctified imagination and celebration, embodying God in colonies of heaven on earth.

Afterword

Now, may

*God be with thee on every hill,
Jesu be with thee in every pass,
Spirit be with thee on every stream,
Headland, ridge, and field;
Each sea and land, each moor and meadow,
In wave trough, on billow crest,
Each step of the journey thou goest.*

(Cadoc's Blessing)

ABOUT THE AUTHOR

Boyd was ordained as a Presbyter (Priest) of the Church with Basileia on December 29, 2004 by Bishops William Paul Mikler and Wayne Boosahda. This book was completed on the eve of his consecration as an Abbot Bishop on January 9, 2016. In ecclesiastical fellowship with *Communio Christiana*,

About the Author

Basileia (which means "kingdom") imagines, cultivates and launches kingdomcultural communities and initiatives, embodying God in colonies of heaven on earth.

Boyd is the founding Abbot of the Basileia Abbey of St. John in Colorado Springs, Colorado and also serves as the Presiding Abbot of the Basileia Alliance. Boyd and his wife, Sheila, happily reside in Colorado Springs. In 2014, Sheila and Boyd co-founded CenterPoint (www.centerpoint.partners).

The Icon of the Resurrection expresses Boyd's passion for Christ and vision for the Church. This image shows Jesus destroying Hades and building His Church. The gates of Hades do not prevail as Christ and His Church destroy evil and restore all things ruined by evil. Christ stands triumphantly upon a figure lying prone in the darkness—the personification of Death, conquered, bound, and defeated. He is building His Church by raising Adam from the dead. Christ defeats Death and the gates of Hades have not prevailed but are now shattered by His descent and have fallen in the form of a cross. Trampling down death by His death, Jesus leaves Hades in utter chaos, littering it with broken locks and chains. Jesus pulls the first man, Adam, from the tomb by his wrist, not by his hand, because Adam cannot help pull himself out of this prison of death. Eve, to the left of Adam, holds her hands out in supplication, waiting for Jesus to raise her too. Various kings, prophets and righteous men who immediately recognize the Risen One look on from the right. Here is pictured the restoration of Adam and all humanity into communion with God. "To earth hast Thou come down, O Master, to save Adam: and not finding him on earth, Thou hast descended into Hades,

Embodying God

seeking him there" (Paschal Matins of the Orthodox Church). Christ's descent into Hades opens the way for all to belong to believe and thereby join the resurrection phenomenon of embodying God in colonies of heaven on earth.

Boyd looks forward to connecting with you at www.basileians.com and hearing from you at bmorris@basileians.com.